SPORTS
12-16

THE
COMPLETE BOOK
OF BALLROOM
DANCING

THE
COMPLETE BOOK
OF BALLROOM
DANCING

Richard M. Stephenson
&
Joseph Iaccarino

DOUBLEDAY
NEW YORK   LONDON   TORONTO   SYDNEY   AUCKLAND

Published by DOUBLEDAY, a division of Bantam Doubleday Dell Publishing Group, Inc., 666 Fifth Avenue, New York, New York 10103.

DOUBLEDAY and the portrayal of an anchor with a dolphin are trademarks of Doubleday, a division of Bantam Doubleday Dell Publishing Group, Inc.

Library of Congress Cataloging in Publication Data
Stephenson, Richard Montgomery, 1917–
    The complete book of ballroom dancing.
    Bibliography: p.
    Includes index.
    1. Ballroom dancing. 2. Ballroom dancing–
History. I. Iaccarino, Joseph, joint author. II. Title.
GV1751.S77   793.3'3   78-22648

ISBN: 0-385-14553-5
Copyright © 1980 by Richard M. Stephenson and Joseph Iaccarino
ALL RIGHTS RESERVED
PRINTED IN THE UNITED STATES OF AMERICA

11   13   15   17   18   16   14   12

CONTENTS

PREFACE vii

I HISTORY OF BALLROOM DANCING 1
  Introduction 3
  Nineteenth-century Changes 9
  Twentieth-century Dancing 24

II BASIC BALLROOM SKILLS, MUSIC AND LANGUAGE 57
  Techniques 58
  Music 68
  Terminology 71

III THE DANCES TODAY 75
  The American Waltz 77
  The Fox-Trot 91
  The Lindy (Swing, Jitterbug, Jive) 105
  The American Rumba 119
  The Cha-Cha 133
  The Mambo 145
  The Tango 157
  The Samba 169
  The Bossa Nova 181
  The Merengue 193
  The Ballroom Polka 203
  The Hustle 215

IV BALLROOM DANCING FOR YOU 229

BIBLIOGRAPHY 239

INDEX 241

PREFACE

One of the most interesting social changes in recent years has been the "return to the ballroom" by students at colleges and universities throughout the United States. In 1974 the authors of this book helped organize the University of Connecticut's Ballroom Dance Club. During the five years the club has been in existence (including three very successful summer workshops), many of our students have pointed out the lack of real help in existing books on ballroom dancing and the need for one that would include a scholarly history of dancing and social attitudes toward it, a basic review of the musical forms associated with ballroom dancing, and detailed instruction in the techniques and skills common to all the dances. This book is the result of our students' observations and requests.

Although the book is intended primarily for beginners, one or two more advanced figures are included in each dance section. In addition, we believe the chapters on history and skills and the advice contained in the final chapter will be of interest to dancers at any level. As often as possible we have gone directly to the original sources for information: contemporary books, newspapers, periodicals, and autobiographies of individuals involved. A search was made of back issues of the New York *Times* and of older periodicals such as *Dance Magazine* and *Dancing Times*. The New York Public Library Theatre and Dance Collections were particularly helpful. Photocopies of certain rare books were supplied by the Library of Congress.

The authors' thanks go to Robin Castellano and Christopher Moon, of the University of Connecticut Ballroom Dance Club, who served as models for the various dances, and to William Beer of Chaplin, Connecticut, who was responsible for the dance photography. John Hall, also of the Dance Club, assisted us in the preparation of the remaining illustrations. The Reference Department of the University of Connecticut Library assisted with interlibrary loans and photostats of certain periodical references.

Particular thanks go to Mary Stephenson who was responsible for the typing, editing, and layout of our entire manuscript. We would also like to thank editors Debra Groisser and Joseph Gonzalez of Doubleday for their encouragement and support throughout the preparation of this book.

Dick Stephenson and Joe Iaccarino

I

HISTORY OF
BALLROOM DANCING

Introduction

Dancing is an integral part of life itself. Certain insects, such as ants and beetles, take part in parades and other activities closely resembling dancing. Male birds don brilliant colors and dance during the mating season; the peacock spreads his tail and struts before the female. Antelopes often dance during mating time; the moose jumps with rhythmic steps about the female he is wooing. The horse was trained to dance after he was domesticated, and the original "horse ballets" were performed for the Romans and Arabs. Anthropoid apes dance, sometimes forming circles and parading around a tree or post. Chimpanzees have been known to bedeck themselves with string, vines, and rags which swing in the air as they move.

Primitive man made dancing the expression of every kind of emotion. Success in the hunt, the birth of a child, marriage and funeral rites, initiation of a young man into the tribe, worship of the gods, and propitiation of evil spirits were all accompanied by appropriate dances. No primitive tribe has been discovered in which dancing was not an important part of the tribal culture.

There is no ancient civilization of which we have record that did not know dancing. Egyptians, Assyrians, Hebrews, Hindus, Greeks, and Romans all danced. In fact, no nation held dancing in higher esteem or cultivated it for its aesthetic values more than the ancient Greeks. To them, dancing not only governed movement of the feet, but also controlled their manner of expression and discipline of the body in its various attitudes.

Roman dancing was initially derived from and hence similar to that of the Greeks. In the latter days of the Roman Empire, it became incredibly coarse, licentious, and degenerate. Credit must be given to the Romans, however, for the development of theatrical dancing, which they brought to a high degree of perfection, and of *pantomime* — an art unknown to the Greeks.

Because of the importance of animals in his daily life, primitive man often practiced animal dances accompanied by special adornment such as a mask, a feathered headdress, or colorful body paint. In medieval times, animal dances continued to be of importance, and some have persisted to our own times. The *pavane* (peacock dance) of the sixteenth century was originally an animal dance. Peasants of Bavaria have a dance called the *hen scratch* as well as the *swallow* and the *dove dance*. In Bohemia, there is the *rak* (crab dance), the *krocan* (turkey dance), and the *zaba* (frog dance). The *cock dance*, which is common throughout Europe, is not only an animal dance but also, at times, a dance of fertility and light.

WHY DO WE DANCE?

Today people dance for one reason only: enjoyment. Social dancing is one of the most important male-female interactions in our society. Knowledge of dancing is a very helpful attribute for a young man or woman starting a career in the business world. It teaches poise, manners, and how to relate comfortably to the opposite sex in a time when sexual freedom is placing increased pressures on our young people. Some of our University of Connecticut students tell us they are amazed at first to find it is possible to come to class, put an arm around a girl and enjoy dancing with her most of the evening, and then say good-bye — each going home without any thought of a sexual relationship.

Dance lessons and dances are a good way for "boy to meet girl" — far better, certainly, than the singles' bars and lounges which are now so prevalent. A survey of married couples in England showed that a large percentage of them had first met on a dance floor. Roseland Dance City in New York City has a roster on the wall of the entrance hall listing hundreds of married couples who first met at Roseland.

Ballroom dancing is good exercise, good fun, and something you can do all your life. As long as you can walk, you can dance. This is particularly important for senior citizens. It provides moderate exercise, an important social outlet, and a way of keeping up with the world. In dancing there is no generation gap, and our college dances are enjoyed by all ages — college freshmen and senior citizens alike.

SOCIAL DANCE

While primitive dances were almost always carried out by members of the same sex with no bodily contact between individual dancers, *social* dance is essentially couple dancing and involves bodily contact ranging from a simple holding of hands to the close embrace of today's "slow dancing." Social dance includes all forms of dancing done primarily for recreation or pleasure. It does not include such performances as the ritual *sword dance* of rural England, ballet, or other professional dancing.

The earliest social dances of which we have any detailed information are the folk and peasant dances of Europe. For example, the *basse* dances (about 1350–1550) and the *pavanes* (about 1450–1650) were formal stately dances done with gliding steps. Both were danced by couples, usually in procession, and they were undoubtedly favored by the nobles and aristocrats of their time.

As early as the fourteenth century, the *round* dance was popular throughout Europe. This was performed by a long chain of dancers holding hands and moving in an open or closed circle or in a long line. Sometimes such "rounds" extended for a long distance, starting in the ballroom and continuing outside into the street with other couples joining the line as it moved.

In England, the country dances (*contredanse*) began in the sixteenth century or before. By the seventeenth century, they were being performed in the Court and remained very popular until about 1820. In seventeenth-century France, the *minuet* was developed by Beauchamps, the leading dancing master of his time. Its name originated from the small (*menu*) steps of the dance. In the early eighteenth-century the *cotillion*, a French folk dance (*cotte* was the short petticoat worn by peasants), was introduced to England and became very popular there.

About 1740 the French also originated a square dance for four couples which came to be known as the *quadrille*. This was presumably derived from one of the folk dances, probably the cotillion. The quadrille was formally introduced into high society in 1816 and became extremely popular. *The Lancers, a Second Set of Quadrilles with Entirely New Figures*, was published in London in 1820. Quadrilles and *lancers* were an important part of dance programs throughout the remainder of the nineteenth century.

Although in the Western Hemisphere there was relatively little ballroom dancing before the nineteenth century, the seeds of Western dancing, particularly of Western dance music, were planted there at an early time. Almost a hundred years before the landing of the Pilgrims in New England, Spaniards in Mexico established schools for the teaching of European music. They began by teaching Indians to copy music neatly and accurately which was the first step in their training as musicians for service with the church. Traditional ballads of Spain were introduced to the New World with the arrival of the first soldiers and colonists. In 1556 the first American-printed music book was published in Mexico City.

Lyric theater played an important part in the spread of Spanish music throughout the Americas. The more successful productions were repeated thousands of times in all the principal cities. Most of the music consisted of popular songs and dances from various regions of Spain. There is much evidence to show that the music of the Argentine tango reached Buenos Aires from Andalusia, Spain, via the lyric theater (*zarzuela*). Some authorities claim that Spanish music engendered nearly all South American music. The basic melodic elements in so-called Afro-Cuban music seem also to be of Hispanic origin, modified by African and Cuban influences.

Development of Spanish music in South America and the West Indies was influenced by four other cultures — Indian, Portuguese, African, and French (Creole). Indian influence was minimal because most of the natives — roughly 90 per cent — were annihilated at a very early date. Portuguese influence was limited pretty much to Brazil, and French influence to the French islands. The influence of the African black was considerable, however. Black slaves of the New World came from many regions of West and West-Central Africa, some from cultures with a high order of music and dance, far advanced over the "monotonous chanting and tom-tom playing" described by early visitors to Africa. There is a strong African element in many of the popular dances of Brazil, such as the *samba*. The *rumba* and the *conga*, two very popular Afro-Cuban dances, show a marked African influence.

A similar situation existed in the United States, where some eight million African blacks were imported as slaves during the seventeenth and eighteenth centuries. Undoubtedly they witnessed Old World social dances in the homes of their white owners and absorbed a great deal from these. It did not take long for the dances to travel from the master's house to the slave quarters, where a new rhythm was introduced. Accent was placed not on the *downbeat*, as in Europe, but on the *upbeat* or offbeat. *Syncopation* was introduced. Tambourines were rattled, bones were clacked, and other devices such as frying pans, washboards, harmonicas, guitars, and banjos were used to make this new, hybrid music.

In the middle of the nineteenth century, there was a tremendous influx of Irish settlers to the United States due to the potato famine at home. Irish "tinkers" traveled everywhere in the South and performed their jigs, clogs, and reels wherever they went. These delighted the blacks, who learned them quickly and added Afro rhythms. The hornpipe and Irish clog were transformed into the buck-and-wing, tap, and the beginnings of jazz dance.

Gradually American blacks developed their own folk dances as well, such as the *buzzard lope, fish tail, camel walk, cake walk, turkey trot, shimmy, bunny hug, Texas twist, walkin' the dog*, etc. Many of these were not names of dances but rather of elements or figures in the dances. Several of these motifs were drawn from African rather than European tradition, and many of the steps, postures, and motifs in these dances were later used in minstrel shows and vaudeville.

BALLROOM DANCING

The term "ballroom dancing" was originally applied to the dances commonly done in a ballroom. The type of dance depended, of course, on the period under consideration. For example, the eighteenth century was primarily the time of open-couple dances, particularly the slow and stately minuet. In France, the minuet and other court dances were killed by the

French Revolution. Even in England, the minuet suffered a gradual decline by the end of the eighteenth century. The face of rural England was becoming more and more industrial; the pace and manner of life were less suitable for a dance such as the minuet, which was gradually being replaced by the contredanse, cotillion, and *allemande*.

The nineteenth century witnessed rapid changes in dancing styles. The minuet had disappeared in the early years of the century, and by 1850 the contredanse (with one exception, the *Sir Roger deCoverley* or *Virginia reel*) was also gone. As these dances declined, the French quadrille became extremely popular. Originally designed for two, four, or any number of couples, it was usually danced in England with four couples. Since the quadrille combined contredanses and cotillions, a large number of figures were possible, thereby lending interest and variety to the dance.

The *waltz* was introduced to fashionable ballrooms in the early nineteenth century. This closed-couple dance with its close hold was at first received with considerable dismay. It was a losing battle, however, and by about 1825 the waltz had come to stay. In 1840, a second closed-couple dance, the *polka*, was introduced to Paris and was feverishly welcomed as a fashionable ballroom dance.

By the early twentieth century, dances such as the *two-step, one-step, fox-trot*, and *tango* had been introduced. Quadrilles, lancers, and other open-couple dances had essentially disappeared, and the usual ballroom dance program consisted entirely of the accepted closed-couple dances.

After the second world war, there was a rapid growth of interest in other forms of dance, such as modern dance, ballet, and square dancing. With the development of rock-and-roll, traditional social dancing went into a decline. In order to prevent confusion, the term "ballroom dancing" came to be used to identify traditional social dancing as contrasted to other forms of dance.

In this book, we shall follow today's accepted practice and assume that ballroom dancing includes the popular closed-couple dances such as the waltz, fox-trot, Lindy, polka, hustle, and the various Latin dances. It does not include square dances, line dances, rock-and-roll, *discothèque*, novelty dances, such as the *Charleston*, or purely ethnic folk dances.

ROUND DANCING

As we have seen, round dancing originally referred to an open-couple dance in which the couples simply joined hands to form a long chain. By the nineteenth century, however, the term was being applied to closed-couple dances. For example, nineteenth century dance books usually had sections on the cotillion, the quadrilles, and the round dances such as the waltz and polka.

During this period of time, round dances became synonymous with sin in the minds of the reformers. Many a Sunday sermon denounced dancing — particularly the "pernicious round dances which have brought heartache to so many homes."

Today the term "round dancing" refers to a structured form of ballroom dancing in which couples form a circle around the room, each doing the same figures at the same time, often with a periodic change of partners. In rural and suburban areas, the term round dancing is still sometimes used to refer to ballroom dancing as opposed to square dancing. For example, only two miles from the University of Connecticut a small private community regularly advertises "Saturday night dancing — round and square."

Nineteenth-century Changes

Class distinctions, still fairly strong at the beginning of the nineteenth century, had an inevitable effect on dancing styles. In Europe, for example, the nobility favored slow, stately dances such as the minuet and cotillion. The peasants continued to do their folk dances, which were gay, lively, and undoubtedly much more fun. Although not much is known of these peasant dances, they were surely much closer to our dancing today. Unhindered by artificial manners, women wore simpler clothing with shorter skirts, and men could hold them tightly without fear of public disgrace. An early description of an Austrian peasant dance states that " . . . the partners had their hands on each other's backs and stood so close together that their faces touched. " This might well be a description of today's "slow dancing."

In both England and the United States, dancing for "society" and dancing for the "working people" were distinctly different. Dancing had always been considered important for the socially prominent, and the local "dancing master" or "professor of dancing" played a prominent role in upper-

"*Le Bal à Bougival*," public dancing in a park near Paris, painted by Pierre Auguste Renoir in 1883. (Courtesy the Boston Museum of Fine Arts)

class society. It is reported that the first dancing master came to New York City as early as 1686 to teach manners to the children of the well-to-do. He didn't last long, and an order of the Council dated January 3, 1687, cites his bad manners and orders him to stop the teaching of dancing. Dancing had attained respectability by the mid-1700s, however, and by 1800 there were seven dancing academies in the city.

During much of the nineteenth century, the Dodworth family set the pace for society dancing in New York City. Allen Dodworth opened his first dance academy in 1842. He stated emphatically that dancing school is not a place of amusement but deals with "matters to do with men's souls." His book, *Dancing and Its Relation to Education and Social Life*, first published in 1885 and in use for more than three decades, was one of the classics in its field. In addition to a description of the dances of the day, it included many pages on proper manners, the *toilette* and the *etiquette* of the ballroom. Much of this book would strike modern readers as rather humorous, such as the advice to gentlemen to remove their hats before dancing, not to make passes at their partners, and not to spit on the floor.

Dancing lessons were given a big boost when Ward McAllister, a social lion of the late nineteenth century, made clear to socially ambitious mothers in New York City the real power of dancing class, i.e., the power to propel their children up the social ladder. He started McAllister's Family Circle Dancing Classes, which were parties by invitation only. Girls of eight or nine wearing pastel dresses and white gloves learned to smile and curtsy; boys of the same age donned blue jackets and ties and learned to ask

Dance Position according to Allen Dodworth, 1885.

a young lady to dance. Dancing class suddenly became synonymous with social success. Every large city needed its "society dance teachers" who never advertised and whose names never appeared in the newspapers.

Dancing in the nineteenth century was strongly influenced by the tremendous economic and social changes that were transforming Western civilization from a rural to a largely urban society. The industrial revolution began in England with the invention of the steam engine in 1760. In 1800 there were twelve cities in England with a population of over 20,000; by 1900 there were nearly two hundred.

In the United States, changes were even more dramatic. The American Revolution stimulated industrial production, which increased rapidly after the Civil War with mass production of standardized articles by machine. Petroleum was discovered in 1859 at Titusville, Pennsylvania, and soon much industry was based on this new source of energy. In 1800 the total population of the United States was 5.3 mllion; three of its cities — Boston, New York, and Philadelphia — had populations of over 25,000. By 1850 the total population was 23 million, and by 1900 this figure had grown to 75 million; thirty-eight cities had populations of over 100,000 at the turn of the century.

Rapid growth of the cities was produced by a migration of young people from rural areas and also by a vast number of immigrants. Living in rooming or boardinghouses, working long hours at a routine machine job, these newcomers — often mere children — had little or no supervision of their personal lives. With no family or friends to provide guidance, they soon forgot their cultural background. There was no entertainment available to them — no television, no radio, no movies. The men could find escape and companionship in the bars and brothels. For the working girls, there was essentially nothing.

In these circumstances, the public dance hall became practically the only source of recreation. In smaller cities, they would serve as centers for community activities such as town meetings, talks by visiting speakers, and dances. In larger cities, the dance halls were strictly commercial. Usually they served liquor and attracted a fairly rough crowd. Inevitably, they were denounced as wicked and immoral; in fact, many clergymen and other reformers considered dancing itself to be sinful.

In 1892 T. A. Faulkner published his book, *From the Ballroom to Hell*, in which he stated that dancing was responsible for 81 per cent of the "fallen women" in Los Angeles. Some years later Mrs. E.M. Whittemore, founder of "The Door of Hope," announced gravely that 70 per cent of the "fallen girls" of New York had been ruined by jazz. In every state of the union there have been periodic investigations, crusades, denunciations, and appeals to Christian indignation blaming dancing for many of the evils of the time.

There is no question that most public halls have never been very wholesome places for "boy meets girl." Many of them catered to a low crowd and attracted customers by obvious sexual suggestion. Some were simply excuses for prostitution, amateur and professional. Particularly bad were the taxi-dance halls or dime-a-dance establishments which flourished from the mid-nineteenth century through the second world war. These were open only to men, who had to take their exercise with "hostesses" or "instructresses" supplied by the manager. The dances were short, often less than a minute. In many cases the trapped male found his partner grabbing seven or eight of his tickets before he realized the first dance had ended. Then came, "You'll have to get some more tickets, dearie," as she pointed to the gate.

The real problem, of course, was the blindness of the community and its indifference to the needs of young people for recreation and joy. The dance hall and dancing itself became the scapegoat for many of the problems of the nineteenth century when, in fact, public dancing fulfilled very real needs of young people caught in a rapidly changing and often bewildering social climate. When the community would finally take action, its attitude was so colored by negative feelings that only repressive legislation resulted, closing down the few places where the public could dance.

DANCING AND THE CHURCH

The Church has had mixed feelings about dancing, encouraging it at times and repressing it at other times. As long as the Catholic Church was the dominant force in Christendom, dancing was encouraged by the heads of that sagacious organization as a useful safety value. The early mystery plays contained choral dances and songs, and some were altogether pageants of dancing. One of these was the well-known *Danse Macabre* or Dance of Death, which later became a popular subject with artists. In this, the frolicsome skeleton extends an invitation to the dance to king, noble, *grand dame*, peasant, child, and beggar alike — all of whom are forced to accept, willy-nilly.

With the first withering blast of the Reformation, dancing became a sin to the devil-chasers of Protestantism. It was seen as a direct threat to the Church itself. Certain sects forbade dancing entirely; others denounced it as immoral. There was always the question, "If people dance on Saturday night, will they go to church on Sunday morning?"

Typical of this attitude toward dancing were the following comments uttered in 1883 by the pastor of Saint Paul's Lutheran Church in New York City:

Dancing has made many homes desolate. It has engendered jealousy in many households; it has ruined many lives and has brought death to many doors. Go to a dancing club, look at the flushed faces, see the attire of the women, mark the looks and gestures of the dancers, hear their words, and then tell me if dancing is God-like. The round dances I look upon as particularly sinful. . . . If you read the reports of the Magdalen asylums, you will see that three-fourths of the young women attribute their downfall to dancing. No husband cares to see his wife in another's arms. . . .

But not all ministers opposed dancing. In 1898, the Reverend John Scudder of the First Congregational Church of Jersey City established a dancing class and commented:

I can see no sin in dancing. . . . To my mind there are three limitations which should be placed on dancing. The first relates to time. Young people should observe proper hours. Dancing after midnight is unhealthy and contrary to nature. . . . The second limitation concerns the manner of dancing. A man should hold his partner at a respectable distance, using his arms to steady and guide her, and the woman should see these instructions are adhered to. When dancing degenerates into a peripatetic hugging, it becomes a disgraceful and sometimes a dangerous pastime. The third limitation is to be careful where and with whom you dance. Confine this amusement as much as possible to the home circle and personal acquaintances. Public halls and dancing pavilions, where young women dance with men they have never seen before, are pernicious in the extreme. . . .

This is pretty good advice — even today.

THE WALTZ

Ballroom dancing as we know it started with the introduction of the *waltz*,* a dance born in the suburbs of Vienna and in the alpine region of Austria. As early as the seventeenth century, waltzes were played in the ballrooms of the Hapsburg court. Even before that time, the turning dances, or *weller*, had been danced by peasants in Austria and Bavaria. Many familiar waltz airs, including Johann Strauss' "The Blue Danube," can be traced back to simple peasant yodeling melodies.

Despite the earlier existence of waltz music, the true waltz period did not begin until the cultural climate was ready for it. By the end of the eighteenth century the transformation of society — so bloody in France, but equally apparent in the rest of Europe — had brought about a revolution in dancing as well. A dance calendar of the year 1801 stated that " . . . the English dances have no character. All they consist of is kicking and

* From the old German word *walzen* meaning to turn, to roll, or to glide.

leaping to the measure, and this is falsely called dancing." The formal and restrained minuets and *gavottes* of the aristocracy were now rejected by this class. Natural and spontaneous dancing became the fashion. With the rise of the new class of industrial workers came a universal demand for freer expression of body movement.

During the middle of the eighteenth century, the *allemande* form of the waltz was very popular in France. Originally danced as one of the figures in the contredanse, with arms intertwining at shoulder level, it soon became an independent dance and the close-hold was introduced. By the end of the eighteenth century, this old Austrian peasant dance had been accepted by high society, and three-quarter rhythm was here to stay.

Opposition to the waltz was not lacking, however, and it came from two quarters. Dancing masters at once saw the waltz as a threat to their profession. The minuet and other court dances required considerable practice, not only to learn the many complex figures, but also to develop suitable postures and deportment. The basic steps of the waltz could be learned in a relatively short time, often just by observation. In 1767 the dancing master Chavanne observed in his *Principes du Menuet* that the waltz had no relation to "*la bonne danse*."

The waltz was also criticized on moral grounds by those opposed to its closer hold and rapid turning movements. Continental court circles held out obstinately against the waltz, and religious leaders almost unanimously regarded it as vulgar and sinful. In England, which had become a land of strict morals, the waltz was accepted even more slowly. Even poets got into the act, with Lord Byron proclaiming:

> Now round the room the circling dow'gers sweep,
> Now in loose waltz the thin-clad daughters leap;
> The first in lengthened line majestic swim.
> The last display the free unfettered limb!
> Those for Hibernia's lusty sons repair
> With arts the charms which nature could not spare;
> Those after husbands wing their eager flight,
> Nor leave much mystery for the nuptial night.

In July of 1816 the waltz was included in a ball given in London by the Prince Regent. Even though none of the Royal Family danced on that occasion, a blistering editorial in *The Times* a few days later stated:

> We remarked with pain that the indecent foreign dance called the Waltz was introduced (we believe for the first time) at the English court on Friday last . . . it is quite sufficient to cast one's eyes on the voluptuous intertwining of the limbs and close compressure on the bodies in their dance, to see that it is indeed far removed from the modest reserve which has hitherto been considered distinctive of

English females. So long as this obscene display was confined to prostitutes and adultresses, we did not think it deserving of notice; but now that it is attempted to be forced on the respectable classes of society by the evil examples of their superiors, we feel it a duty to warn every parent against exposing his daughter to so fatal a contagion. . . . We know not how it has happened (probably by the recommendation of some worthless and ignorant French dancing-master) that so indecent a dance has how been exhibited at the English court . . . we trust it will never again be tolerated in any moral English society.

Even as late as 1866 an article in the English magazine *Belgravia* stated:

We who go forth of nights and see without the slightest discomposure our sister and our wife seized on by a strange man and subjected to violent embraces and canterings round a small-sized apartment — the only apparent excuse for such treatment being that it is done to the sound of music — can scarcely realize the horror which greeted the introduction of this wicked dance. It, of course, came from France; and a few of the older caricatures and social skits of the time will show how shocked, almost *écrasée*, was the maternal instinct of the day. . . .

But the result of all this antagonism was only an increase in the popularity of the waltz. The *bourgeoisie* took it up enthusiastically immediately after the French Revolution. By the close of the eighteenth century it was reported that Paris alone had nearly seven hundred dance halls. A German traveler to Paris in 1804 stated, "This love for the waltz and this adoption of the German dance is quite new and has become one of the vulgar fashions since the war, like smoking." The young people of Paris merely replied, *"Une valse, ah, encore une valse!"*

It is not known exactly when the waltz was introduced to the United States. Reportedly, it was first danced in Boston in 1834, when Lorenzo Papanti, a Boston dancing master, gave an exhibition in Mrs. Otis' Beacon Hill mansion. Social leaders were aghast at what they called "an indecorous exhibition." It was probably brought to New York and Philadelphia at about the same time, and by the middle of the nineteenth century was firmly established in United States society.

Every dance is dependent upon the availability of appropriate music. Beginning about 1830 the waltz was given a tremendous boost by two great Austrian composers, Franz Lanner and Johann Strauss, the younger. They were by far the most popular composers of dance music during the nineteenth century, and they set the standard for the Viennese waltz, a very fast version played at about 55–60, measures per minute. By 1900 a typical dance program was three quarters waltzes and one quarter all other dances combined.

The fast tempo of the Viennese waltz did indeed present problems.

Much of the enjoyment of the new dance was lost in the continual strain to keep up with the music. This led to development of the *valse à deux temps*, which became quite popular around the 1850s. The name itself was confusing and should have been *valse à deux pas* (waltz with two steps), since the dance consisted of taking two steps to the three beats of each waltz measure.

Around the close of the nineteenth century, two modifications of the waltz developed in the United States. The first was the *Boston*, a slower waltz with long gliding steps; there were fewer and slower turns and more forward and backward movement than in the Viennese waltz. Although the *Boston* disappeared with the first world war, it did stimulate development of the English or International style which continues today. The second modification was the *hesitation*, which involves taking one step to three beats of the measure. *Hesitation* steps are still widely used in our faster waltzes.

Another factor contributing to modification of the Viennese waltz was the continuing trend toward more natural body movement. Throughout the nineteenth century, dancing masters had insisted that all dances be done with the feet in turned-out position. This was fine for the rapid rotations of the Viennese waltz and gave dancers an opportunity to display the excellence of their footwork. But by the end of the nineteenth century dancing in England and the United States was becoming less stylized, with more forward-and-back movement and with the feet comfortably positioned as for walking. Newer dances such as the *two-step* were introduced, and these called for an entirely new style of dancing.

It is of interest to note that ballroom dance books of the nineteenth century invariably start with a description of the "five positions" for dancing. These all involved a turning out of one foot or both and were used as a basis to describe the movement of the feet while dancing. Although this terminology has now been dropped in ballroom dancing, it is still an important part of ballet and modern dance.

THE POLKA

There appears to be no question that the *polka* was originally a Czech peasant dance, developed in eastern Bohemia (now part of Czechoslovakia). Though it is possible that the polka evolved from one of the many Czech folk dances, Bohemian historians believe that it was invented by a peasant girl one Sunday for her amusement. The village teacher wrote down the actual music and the dance was later performed at the village festivals. In 1833 this dance was first introduced into the ballrooms of

LA
DANSE

DES

SALONS,

PAR CELLARIUS,

DESSINS DE GAVARNI, — GRAVÉS PAR LAVIEILLE.

Deuxième Édition.

PARIS,

CHEZ L'AUTEUR, RUE NEUVE-VIVIENNE, 49,

ET CHEZ LES PRINCIPAUX LIBRAIRES.

1849

Title page from *La Danse des Salons* by Cellarius, which served as the basis for practically all ballroom dance instruction during the second half of the nineteenth century.

Prague. The name of the dance (*pulka*) is Czech for "half-step," referring to the rapid shift from one foot to the other.

In 1840 Raab, a dancing teacher of Prague, danced the polka at the Odéon Theatre in Paris where it was a tremendous success. Parisian dancing teachers seized on the new dance and refined it for their salons and ballrooms. According to Cellarius, the famous French dancing master of the mid-nineteenth century: "What young man is there, although formerly most opposed to dancing, whom the polka has not snatched from his apathy to acquire, willy-nilly, a talent suddenly become indispensable?" A veritable polkamania resulted. Dance academies were swamped and in desperation recruited ballet girls from the Paris Opéra as dancing partners to help teach the polka. This move naturally attracted many young men who were interested in things other than dancing, and manners and morals in the dance pavilions deteriorated. Dancing developed a bad name, and many parents forbade their daughters dancing with any but close friends of the family.

By the middle of the nineteenth century, the polka was introduced in England, but never achieved there the popularity it had attained on the Continent. By this time also, it had reached the United States, and Thomas Balch, in his book *Philadelphia Assemblies*, reports that Breiter's band composed a new polka for the occasion of the 1849 Assembly. It was evident the waltz and polka were gradually replacing the contredanse and cotillion.

The great popularity of the polka led to the introduction of several other dances from central Europe. The simplest was the *galop* or *galoppade* which was introduced into England and France in 1829. One of the earliest references to this dance was a book by Joseph Franken, *Die galoppade, wie sie getanzt werden soll*, published in Cologne in 1829. Dance position was the same as for the waltz or polka, with couples doing a series of fast *chassés* about the room, with occasional turns. Music was in 2/4 time, often merely a fast polka. The galop was particularly popular as the final dance of the evening.

The *polonaise*, named for its country of origin, was a stately processional march in slow 3/4 time, often used for the opening of a fancy-dress ball. It never achieved, however, great popularity as a ballroom dance. The Bohemian *redowa* consisted of three successive movements: a "pursuit" step, an ordinary waltz step, and a *valse à deux temps* step. It was danced to a slow waltz. The Polish *mazurka*, a fairly complicated dance to waltz music, included hops, sliding steps, and kicking the heels together. The *schottische* was a German folk dance that consisted of a series of chassés and hops done to 2/4 and 4/4 music. There were also combination dances such as the polka-redowa and polka-mazurka. In addition, many figures from these dances were incorporated into the quadrilles, such as the polka-quadrille and mazurka-quadrille.

Of all the ballroom dances originating in the nineteenth-century, the only one that has survived is the polka. After the initial enthusiasm, the polka gradually declined in popularity and reached a low point with the introduction of ragtime, jazz, and the newer dances of the early twentieth century. After the second world war, however, Polish immigrants to the United States adopted the polka as their "national" dance, and it is now extremely popular not only with them but also with many other Americans who have succumbed to the new polka craze popularized by Lawrence Welk and other post-war bands.

THE TWO-STEP

From about 1890 to 1920, one of the most popular dances in the United States was the *two-step*. This was a natural development from the *valse à deux temps*, popular in the middle of the nineteenth century. The dance consisted of a series of chassés either forward or sideward to 2/4 or 4/4 music.

In 1891 John Philip Sousa composed one of his most popular marches, the "Washington Post March." The new music had a lively beat and became very popular. The two-step which was danced to it was simply a quick march with a skip in each step. In 1894 the Washington Post two-step came to England and was quite popular for a short time.

The two-step gradually declined in popularity during the early years of the twentieth century and essentially disappeared during the jazz era. However, some figures were incorporated into the fox-trot and survive in this form.

TYPICAL DANCE PROGRAMS

What were people actually dancing in the nineteenth century? In London, there were popular "assembly rooms" which were very fashionable at one time but gradually became less exclusive. P.J.S. Richardson in *Social Dances of the 19th Century*, gives a typical program for an evening at Laurent's Casino, which had dancing from seven to eleven-thirty with an admission charge of one shilling:

From 1894 to 1920, *The Two Step* reported the activities of dance teachers in the United States.

1.	Quadrille (first set)	"Robert Bruce"	Musard
2.	Polka	"Souvenir de l'Hippodrome"	Fessy
3.	Valse	"Pas des Fleurs"	Maratzek
4.	Parisian Quadrille	"Le Comte de Carmagnola"	Bosisio
5.	Cellarius Valse	"New National Mazurkas"	Sapinsky
6.	Parisian Quadrille	"Don Pasquale"	Tolbecque
7.	Polka	"Eclipse"	Koenig
8.	Valse	"Le Romantique"	Lanner
9.	Parisian Quadrille	"Nino"	Coote
10.	Polka	"Polka d'Amour"	Wallenstein
11.	Parisian Quadrille	"Les Fêtes du Chateau d'Eu"	Musard
12.	Polka	"Les Amazones"	Val Morris

Dance programs in the United States were not greatly different. For example, in 1871 the Grand Duke Alexis of Russia visited New York City and was received at a grand ball at the Academy of Music. The dance program, as printed in the New York *Times*, was probably typical for a large society function:

Polonaise de Reception   Julian

1.	Lancers	"Les Brigands"	Downing
2.	Valse	"Weiner Kinder"	Strauss
3.	Galop	"Position d'Amour"	Hermann
4.	Quadrille	"Semiramis"	Jullien
5.	Valse	"Amorettentanze"	Gung'l
6.	Lancers	"Concordia"	Hartung
7.	Valse	"Casino"	Gung'l
8.	Galop	"Petersburg Champagne"	Lumbye
9.	Russian Quadrille	"Zolotage Rybka"	Minkne
10.	Galop	"Il Crescendo"	Jullien
11.	Lancers	"Faust"	Gounod
12.	Valse	"Deutscher Hertzen"	Strauss
13.	Galop	"Genevieve"	Offenbach
14.	Quadrille	"Prince Alexis"	Eben
15.	Galop	"Glocken Spiel"	Labitzky
16.	Lancers	"Cloches de l'Hermite"	Wiegand
17.	Valse	"St. Petersburg"	Louna
18.	Galop	"Ekaterinburg"	Jullien
19.	Polka Redowa	"Love's Bouquet"	Parlott
20.	Valse	"Thousand and One Nights"	Strauss

During the latter half of the nineteenth century, fashionable balls and masquerades became extremely popular in the United States. In New York City, large balls were sponsored by such groups as the Catholic Orphan Asylum, Cercle Français, Charity, Fireman's, Knights of Pythias, Ihpatonga of Brooklyn, Matriarch's Assembly, Palestine Commandery, Tuesday Evening Dancing Class, Yorkville Brewers' Battalion, and so forth. These were often very large affairs, involving two or three thousand people and a dance band comprising a hundred pieces or more.

Even more humble groups had their balls. For example, the New York *Times* of November 26, 1870, reported: "The twentieth annual ball of the Journeymen's Horse-shoeing and Protective Union Benevolent Society took place last night at Apollo Hall and was most numerously attended. No one could be mistaken as to the nationality of those present, all or nearly all being natives of the Emerald Isle."

By the end of the nineteenth century, however, large balls had almost entirely disappeared, victims of their gross extravagance. For several years newspapers had reported caustically that these "social pleasurings" had become the most expensive diversions of fashionable society. The average cost of a Patriarch ball had increased to over six thousand dollars, and a prominent florist reported that at least eight hundred thousand dollars would be spent on American Beauty roses by the opening of the Lenten season. By 1900, dancing was indeed at a low ebb.

Except for the costumes, ballroom dancing has changed relatively little in over one hundred years. Drawing from *Harper's Weekly*, February 20, 1858.

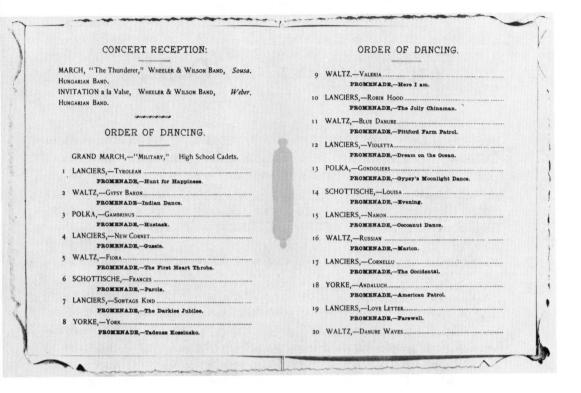

A typical dance program, February 2, 1893.

Twentieth-century Dancing

The start of the twentieth century witnessed an extremely important development in American dance music: ragtime. Songs of the nineteenth century tended to be prim and sentimental. These were intended for the home piano, the only kind of home music available at that time. Only ladies played the piano, and they were always pictured as sweet and innocent. Magazines such as *Godey's Ladies' Book* printed original songs and gave advice on manners and fashion. There was also a good market for song sheets, many of which were fairly elaborate, often hand-colored works of art.

Ragtime revolutionized dancing and set audiences heel-tapping to a new kind of rhythm. "You just can't sit still when the band plays a rag!" Ragtime was created by southern blacks, most of them poor and without formal education. They played their music in saloons, bars, brothels and cafes — any place where wine, women and song could liven up an otherwise drab existence. Much of the music was never written down or recorded, and even those who had the foresight to market their compositions often received very little in return.

Ragtime was essentially piano music based on conventional European marches and dance rhythms, usually in 2/4 time. The new feature of ragtime was persistent syncopation in the melody line achieved by delaying or advancing a melodic note for half a beat while maintaining a regular uniform beat with the left hand. The melodic shifts were very similar to those found in earlier minstrel shows. The name was originated by people going into music stores and asking for more of that "ragged" music.

Syncopation was not entirely new, since it had been used by Mozart, Beethoven, Brahms, and other European composers. However, persistent syncopation in dance music was new. Ragtime was the product of many composers, but the name most closely associated with early ragtime was that of Scott Joplin. Born in Texarkana, Texas, in 1868, Joplin acquired some musical training from a German music teacher in his town. In 1885, he went to St. Louis and played in "Honest John" Turpin's Silver Dollar Saloon, where he met many other black musicians of the day. Ten years later he moved to Sedalia, Missouri, and began composing the rags (among which the "Maple Leaf Rag," his most important song) which were to establish his fame. "The Entertainer," written in 1902, was recently used in the movie *The Sting*, which helped trigger the current ragtime revival.

In spite of his great musical success, Joplin did not achieve happiness in his life. His first marriage was a failure, and his last years were spent on a ragtime opera which had only one performance during his lifetime. He died in 1917 in a mental home, a lonely and forgotten figure.

RAGTIME DANCES

The increasing popularity of fast ragtime music necessitated a change in dancing styles, and people were ready for such a change. Class distinctions were crumbling steadily as a result of rapid industrial growth. Better working conditions led to the rise of an increasingly important class of professionals and skilled labor. Society was slowly recognizing an obligation to do something for the ordinary worker. In New York City, several social leaders established a Committee on Amusements and Vacation Resources for Working Girls, which was active in the investigation of dance halls and other facilities used by young people. Relations between the sexes became easier and less formal.

The first ragtime dance to be introduced was the *one-step*, a constant-tempo dance with one step taken to each beat of the music. It was ideal for a fast rag or a march. A version of the one-step which achieved particular popularity was the Castle Walk, introduced by Vernon and Irene Castle about 1912.

In the same year, a musical show called *Over the River* reached New York from San Francisco. It featured a dance called the *turkey trot*, which was basically a fast one-step with arms pumping at the sides and occasional arm-flapping like a crazed turkey. There was also a song called "Everybody's Doing It," which had the repeated phrase, "It's a bear!" — at which point the dancers were supposed to lurch like a grizzly bear.

Suddenly young people throughout the United States were doing the turkey trot and other dances such as the *grizzly bear, bunny hug, Boston dip, shiver dance, lovers' two-step, hug-me-close,* and *Gaby glide*. The attraction of these new dances is simple to comprehend. The "impeccable" waltz as taught by the dancing teachers was so fast you were lucky to hold onto your partner in any way you could. The new dances, however, were slower and permitted what was denounced as "lingering close contact." Furthermore, they were so simple that anyone could learn them just by observation in an evening of dancing. Thus, in describing the new dances, a visitor from England said, "As far as I can see, all you have to do is grab hold of the nearest lady, grasp her very tightly, push her shoulders down a bit, and then wiggle about as much like a slippery slush as you possibly can."

Pinpointing the origins of these dances is difficult. For years the blacks of the South had been doing folk dances with names such as *turkey trot, grizzly bear*, and *shimmy*; however, it is very unlikely that the dances of the early twentieth century were based in any way on the black dances. A commonly offered explanation was that these dances originated in the brothels of the Barbary Coast in San Francisco and spread from there to local bars and public dance halls. This is not a very creditable theory, however, since it was offered by people who felt that a brothel was the only possible place where these "sinful" dances could have originated.

Be that as it may, many considered turkey-trotting synonymous with "trotting to Hell." Edward Bok, editor of the *Ladies' Home Journal*, summarily fired fifteen of his office girls for dancing the turkey trot at lunchtime. Several members of the Methodist Episcopal Church at Clayton, New Jersey, threatened to resign because their pastor called dancing "hugging to music" and threatened to dismiss church members who danced. A special meeting of six hundred society people, social workers, clergymen, and city officials was held at Delmonico's Restaurant in New York City where exhibitions were given of the turkey trot and other new dances. They shuddered at the *shiver*, gasped at the *bunny hug* and denounced cheek-to-cheek dancing.

Particularly interesting was the reaction of dance teachers to the new vogue. Publicly they condemned the dances, yet in a short while they were offering lessons in the turkey trot — often a "purified" version. T. George Dodworth, a well-known society dance teacher and son of Allen Dodworth commented:

> The real objection is to what is done in the one-step, which is a modified turkey trot shorn of the shoulder and waist wriggle. Even so, there is no objection to the step itself, which is practically just a promenade, but simply to the manner of holding partners. The young dance it so close together that it would be impossible to get even a sheet of paper between them. They learned it from their elders, and they simply added greater eccentricities and abandon of their own accord. The young dancers simply take advantage of the dances to embrace. Recently I have had girls tell me that the closer they hug their partners the more popular they are at dances. . . .

In a vain attempt to enforce dancing modesty, various mechanical devices, called "bumpers," were developed to maintain a respectable distance between the two partners. At an international conference of dancing masters in Paris, Professor Ross of Rouen demonstrated his "Princess Lily Girdle." This consisted of a broad belt worn about a lady's waist and containing a special band of corset steel in which were fixed three metallic pointed studs to keep the male partner at a proper distance. The Princess Lily met with the highest approval from the clergy and from medical men. From the lay press, however, came nothing but derision; one writer suggested that the girdle, after proper exposition in the Rue de la Paix as an idiosyncrasy of the age, be consigned to the Cluny Museum where it would have as company many famous *ceintures* dating from the Crusades.

All this concern about the turkey trot was, of course, a waste of time. It did nothing to change the minds of those doing the dance, and a few years later it faded from the scene. The one-step lasted a little longer, but by about 1930 it, too, was essentially gone. Certain figures of the one-step were incorporated into the *fox-trot*, and the *Peabody* — essentially a fast one-step — is still a popular dance.

THE TANGO

The *tango* originated in Spain, was brought to the New World by Spanish settlers, and then returned to the mother country modified by black and Creole influences. In the early nineteenth century, the Andalusian (Spanish) tango was a solo dance for a woman and had nothing in common with the tango of today except certain rhythmical elements. Later the Andalusian tango was done by one or two couples walking together, using castanets. In this form it achieved popularity from about 1850 to 1875. By 1900 the tango had come into disfavor with many of the dancing teachers because it was considered "flirting" music and an immoral dance.

It is generally agreed that the ballroom tango originated among the lower classes in Buenos Aires, Argentina, during the nineteenth century. It was particularly popular in the ill-famed *Barrio de las Ranas*, the most disreputable section of the city. The girls wore full skirts and the men wore gaucho costumes with high boots and spurs; dancing in this cumbersome outfit brought about several movements which are today characteristic of the tango. The dance was called the *baile con corté*, the "dance with a stop".

When the gallants of the town saw this dance, they introduced it to their own cafés, which were also of doubtful respectability. In order to produce a more dreamy effect, they substituted the *habañera* rhythm and, to show it was no longer the common *baile con corté*, they called it the *tango*. In this form, the dance was introduced into Spain in the late nineteenth century and into France at about the turn of the century. In 1912, the tango was introduced into England and immediately became extremely popular there.

Although an 1856 American dance book describes a ballroom modification of the tango ("originally a South American dance composed in two-fourth time, arranged for the ball-room by M. Markowski") the dance was essentially unknown in the United States until it was popularized by Maurice Mouvet in the winter of 1910–11. Maurice was a New Yorker born in 1889 of Belgian parents. At the age of fourteen, he was taken to Paris by his father where, on his own, he learned dancing in the Parisian cafes. One evening at the Café de Paris, a party of South Americans were dancing the Argentine tango. Maurice was fascinated by the dance, and soon he and his partner had incorporated the basic tango figures into their routine.

In 1911 Maurice and his partner returned to New York where they gave exhibitions of the tango and the *apache* dance at Louis Martin's Restaurant,

The first reference to the tango as a ballroom dance. From *The Fashionable Dancer's Casket* by Charles Durang, Fisher and Brothers, Philadelphia, 1856.

which soon became very popular among fashionable New Yorkers. Maurice opened a dancing studio, charging $25 an hour for lessons, and obtained a dancing part in the musical comedy, *Over the River*. It was while performing in this musical that Maurice found a new partner, Florence Walton, whom he later married. They danced together for several years, touring all over Europe and the United States.

Meanwhile, the United States was engulfed in a dance fever that peaked in 1913 and 1914. By 1914 New York City alone had some seven hundred dance halls, studios, academies, *jardins* and places where one could dance from noon until dawn of the next day. There were tea dances, tango teas, and society *thé dansants*. Even a man with a two-by-four concession on the Boardwalk at Coney Island had to cut down on the size of his lemonade stand and put in a dancing floor.

Dancing was so popular it made heavy inroads in theatrical receipts. Ballroom dancers appeared in practically every musical show. New York had a musical comedy entitled *The Tango Doctor* and, not to be outdone, Philadelphia put on *The Tango Teacher*, a comedy about a girl who falls in love with a dance teacher. The Fifth Avenue Theater in New York installed a dance floor and let its audiences dance during intermissions, with music and refreshments provided *gratis* by the management.

The Mississippi Pearl Button Company of Burlington, Iowa, filed an injunction to forbid calliope music on the river steamboats during working hours. When the calliopes played tango music, the two hundred girls employed there refused to work. In Atlantic City, New Jersey, Mrs. Lillian Albers, soloist of St. Paul's Methodist Episcopal Church choir, received an ultimatum: Stop teaching the tango or resign from the choir. She resigned immediately. The Reverend W. H. Bromley, a visiting evangelist, then preached a sermon declaring drink to be first and the dance next as causes of immorality.

By 1914 the dancing craze was beginning to ebb — and with it the popularity of the society dancer. Dance halls were acquiring a bad name, particularly those in the "tango district" of New York. Wives visited these places while their husbands presumably worked. Always a crowd of male idlers hung around, and the women who dropped in for excitement usually found it. Although the functions were called tango teas, the neophyte soon saw that tea-cups were seldom used. One of the waiters when questioned by a visitor said, "Oh, sir, we seldom serve tea. They wiggle much better on whisky!" Actually, most women preferred cocktails, many of which bore the names of favorite dancers.

The young men who patronized these dance halls were known as "lounge lizards" and later as "gigolos." They were delighted to have bored wives buy them drinks and give them money in return for romantic favors. When a few turned to blackmail, however, it was the beginning of the end. Husbands ordered their wives — and brothers told their sisters — to keep away from matinée dancing. The dance craze ended as rapidly as it began, leaving in its trail a collection of broken homes, bankrupt restaurants, and unemployed dance teachers.

In spite of the collapse of dancing in 1914, the tango survived as a ballroom dance. Interestingly enough, it was not at that time considered a respectable dance in the country of its birth. Thus, when Paris went tango mad, inquiries at the Argentine embassy produced surprised looks and a remark that any woman doing the tango in Argentina would be considered "suspect."

The ballroom tango of 1914 was entirely different from today's dance. Dance teachers were continually developing new figures, and there was no attempt to standardize the dance. It got so bad that one newspaper columnist reported that there could be found a new tango step for each day of the year!

After the first world war, the tango was simplified and standardized. The throbbing *habanera* music was replaced by the more subdued *milonga* music, normally played in 2/4 time. *Contrary body movement* and the tango *draw* were introduced. About 1930 there was a rebirth of interest in exhibition ballroom dancing, and couples such as Veloz and Yolanda gave exhibitions of Latin dancing which stimulated new interest in the tango. Even Argentina accepted the tango as a proper society dance, and for ballroom dancers of today, this first Latin dance is still very much alive and well!

VERNON AND IRENE CASTLE

Interest in ballroom dancing prior to the first world war was given a tremendous boost by Vernon and Irene Castle. Born in England in 1887, Vernon Blyth received a degree in engineering from Birmingham University and shortly afterward came to New York with his father for a holiday. His sister was an actress and having nothing else to do, Vernon attended rehearsals and was given a small part. He adopted the stage name Castle and appeared with some success in several successive productions by Lew Fields. In 1911 he married Irene Foote, who had played a small part in one of the Fields shows. Shortly thereafter they went to Paris to take part in a musical show; however, the show never opened, and in desperation they turned to exhibition dancing. They were befriended by "Papa Louis," owner of the Café de Paris, who arranged for them to give nightly exhibitions in his restaurant. After a year in Paris, however, Irene became homesick, and they returned to New York in 1912 — just in time to take part in the coming dance craze.

For the next two years, the Castles were the most publicized dance team in the world. Adopted by New York society, they commanded fantastic prices for dance lessons and exhibitions. Elizabeth Marbury and other social leaders established Castle House as a suitable studio for *thé dansants* and lessons in "refined" dancing, and music was provided by the Castle House Orchestra. Mrs. Marbury also published the book *Modern Dancing*, by "Mr. and Mrs. Vernon Castle," which described the dances that met the approval of the famous dancing couple; namely, the *one-step, hesitation waltz, tango*, and *maxixe*. Castle Park was established at Coney Island so that vacationing New Yorkers could keep up with their dance lessons. There was a Castle Club, of which Vernon was president, and Castles-by-the-Sea at then-elegant Long Beach. In 1914 they appeared together in the Charles Dillingham musical *Watch Your Step*, with songs written by Irving Berlin especially for them. In 1915 they were featured at Castles in the Air, the roof-garden of the Forty-Fourth Street Theatre, at a salary of $1,500 a week!

Irene Castle set the styles in dress as well as dancing. She told women to throw away their boned corsets and hobble skirts — dancing should be free and unhampered. When Irene bobbed her hair, suddenly all the women of

America demanded bobbed hair. When Irene gave her approval to a dance, it automatically acquired the badge of respectability.

By 1915, however, the dance craze was coming to an end, and New York society was losing interest in the Castles. Also, Vernon was tiring of the life and — still a British subject — he was concerned about the war in Europe. In 1916 Vernon abandoned dancing for aviation and became a lieutenant in the Royal Flying Corps. After surviving two years over the German lines with only a minor wound, he was killed early in 1918 in an airplane crash in Texas where he had been sent to train American pilots.

After Vernon's death, Irene Castle appeared in several musical shows and also made a few movies. She was not a good business woman, however, and lost a large part of the money she and Vernon had made from dancing. She remarried three times, and after her third marriage in 1923, Irene abandoned the stage and devoted the rest of her life to her concern for animals.

DANCING COSTUME

Social dancing has never required its own costume — both men and women simply wear the customary evening dress or "ball dress" of the times. Early dance teachers were reluctant to give any advice on dress to women, sometimes merely suggesting that they wear something light with not too long a skirt. As for the men, a dance book of 1867 gave the following advice:

> The dress should be studiously neat, leaving no impression than that of a well-dressed gentleman. Black dress coat, black or white vest, black trowsers, white necktie, patent leather boots or pumps and black or white stockings, white kid gloves, hair well dressed. Coats of fancy character and colors, velvet collars, and metal buttons are not proper for the opera or ball.

The nineteenth-century costume for men was not too uncomfortable, although as late as the first world war a gentleman always wore a starched shirt front and a high, stiff turnover collar with the necktie emerging at the bottom of a narrow opening between flaps. However, this was nothing compared to the tortures borne by women: high whale-boned corsets, tight lacing, street-sweeping skirts, trains dragging behind, and later the bustle and hobble skirt. Small wonder that slow stately dances were favored by society ladies while fast polkas and galops were left for the public dance halls.

Irene Castle in the book *Modern Dancing* (1914) was the first to rebel against the fashions of the day. Her first suggestion was to forget whalebone and substitute an elastic "Castle Corset" designed especially for dancing. A pleated petticoat with lace or rosebud trimming was suggested to hide the ankles while doing a dip; silk stockings with at most two pairs of garters, silk bloomers, and a new French garment called a *brassière* were to complete the underpinnings. For a tea dance, an ordinary skirt and loose blouse were appropriate. In the evening, a gown of "something soft and light" was recommended, with a flared ankle-length skirt, fullness over the hips and looseness in the sleeves to prevent binding when the arms were raised. A simple coiffure, small hat, and comfortable shoes, such as pumps with a moderate heel, large enough to dance in and held firmly in place with ribbons, completed the costume.

When the United State entered the first world war in 1917, "helping the boys overseas" became respectable and patriotic. Large numbers of women volunteered for war work where comfortable and practical costume was essential. The end of the war brought the Roaring Twenties: hemlines suddenly rose to the knee, and the clothing rebellion of women was now completed.

Today there is a much wider choice of costume available, but the same general rules apply. Dancing is active exercise, and loose, cool, comfortable clothing is desirable for both sexes. Comfortable leather-soled shoes are a must — particularly for women to properly execute their turns and pivots. There is no need for discomfort on the dance floor!

THE FOX-TROT

During the first few months of 1914, the New York *Times* covered three conventions of dance teachers, and in no case was the *fox-trot* even mentioned. But by the end of the summer, practically all the teachers in New York were advertising lessons in the fox-trot. On September 3, 1914, the American Society of Professors of Dancing proposed to standardize the steps of the popular dances of the day — including the fox-trot!

The first published reference to the fox-trot was an advertisement in the New York *Times* of July 26, 1914, announcing lessons in the new dance by G. Hepburn Wilson, M.B. Wilson owned three small dance studios in New York and was the first dance master to advertise widely and to offer individual rather than group lessons. For a brief time, Arthur Murray was one of his teachers. The M.B. after Wilson's name was supposed to stand for Master of Ballet, but his employees referred to him behind his back as "More Bull."

There is no question but that the fox-trot was originated in the summer of 1914 by the vaudeville actor Harry Fox. Born in Pomona, California, in 1882, Fox was the son of an actor and the grandson of George L. Fox, the celebrated clown. Harry's real name was Arthur Carringford, but he adopted the stage name of "Fox" after his grandfather. At the age of fifteen Harry was thrown on his own resources and joined a circus for a

The first published reference to the fox-trot. From the New York *Times*, July 26, 1914.

brief tour. He played professional baseball for a short while, but a music publisher liked his voice and hired him to sing songs from the boxes of vaudeville theaters in San Francisco. He was soon appearing regularly in vaudeville and became an entertainer in cabarets of the Barbary Coast. In 1904 he appeared at the Belvedere Theatre in a comedy entitled *Mr. Frisky of Frisco*. After the San Francisco earthquake and fire of 1906, Harry Fox migrated East, with stops in Chicago and finally New York.

His first New York engagements were booked through a burlesque promoter who set him to work with the "Miner Burlesquers." After four seasons, he had his own show, *Harry Fox's Merry's*, which was followed by a part in *The Pet of the Petticoats* and his first vaudeville tour. In 1912 and 1913, Fox appeared in two musicals, *The Passing Show of 1912* and the very successful *The Honeymoon Express*.

In early 1914 Fox was appearing in various vaudeville shows in the New York area. In April of that year he teamed up with Yansci Dolly of the famous Dolly sisters in an act at Hammerstein's. At the same time, the New York Theatre, one of the largest in the world, was being converted into a movie house. As an extra attraction for its customers, the theater's management decided to try vaudeville acts between the shows, and, because of the interest in ballroom dancing, they selected Harry Fox and his company of "American Beauties" to put on a dancing act. An article in *Variety*

Harry Fox. (Theatre Collection; the New York Public Library at Lincoln Center; Astor, Lenox and Tilden Foundations)

Magazine stated, "Harry Fox will appear for a month or longer at a large salary with billing that will occupy the front of the theatre in electrics." At the same time, the roof of the theater was converted to a *Jardin de Danse*, and the Dolly Sisters were featured in a nightly revue.

The May 29, 1914, issue of *Variety Magazine* reported "The debut of Harry Fox as a lone star and act amidst the films of the daily change at the New York Theatre started off with every mark of success. The Dolly Sisters are dancing nightly on the New York Roof. Gold cups will be given away next week to the winners of dance contests on the New York Roof." The New York *Times* reported that Harry Fox was doing his dances and songs supported by a bevy of "American Beauties."

The fox-trot originated in the *Jardin de Danse* on the roof of the New York Theatre. As part of his act downstairs, Harry Fox was doing trotting steps to ragtime music, and people referred to his dance as "Fox's Trot." Wishing to capitalize on this, the management introduced the dance at the roof garden. Harry Fox was undoubtedly spending considerable time in the *Jardin de Danse*, since he and Yansci Dolly were "making plans"; in fact, they were married at Long Beach, Long Island, in August of that year. Thus it is quite plausible that he cooperated with her in the introduction of the dance to patrons on the roof.

From the New York *Times*, May 24, 1914.

From the New York *Times*, June 21, 1914.

This version of the origin of the fox-trot is essentially that given in 1951 by Oscar Duryea, a well-known dance teacher. Of even more significance is a brief story published in the November 1914 issue of a British periodical, *Dancing Times*. This quotes an article by F. Leslie Clendennen, a dance teacher from St. Louis, which states that the fox-trot is " ... a nerve-wracking movement arranged by a vaudeville actor named Fox — only a few weeks ago Mr. Fox was showing his original trot."

Ironically, neither fame, fortune, nor happiness resulted for those who developed today's most popular dance. In 1917 Yansci filed suit for divorce. On October 26, 1921, the New York *Times* ran a brief note announcing that "Harry Fox, actor, of 110 West 48th Street filed a petition in bankruptcy yesterday, listing liabilities of $17,777 and no assets." Fox's second and third marriages (to Florrie Millership of vaudeville's Millership Sisters, and to Beatrice Curtis, his sometime co-star and mother of his only son) also ended in divorce. Fox eventually drifted to Hollywood where he obtained only bit parts and where he was married once again, this time to actress Evelyn Brent. He died on July 20, 1959, at the Motion Picture Rest Home and Hospital near Hollywood.

Yansci Dolly's career also went downhill after her divorce from Fox. She and her sister Roszika made one movie, *The Great Dolly Sisters*, but gradually disappeared after that. Yansci died June 1, 1941 — a suicide by hanging.

The fox-trot was the most significant development in all of ballroom dancing. The combination of quick and slow steps permits more flexibility and gives much greater dancing pleasure than the monotonous one-step and two-step which it has replaced. There is more variety in the fox-trot than in any other dance, and in some ways it is the hardest dance to learn.

Variations of the fox-trot include, the *Peabody*, the *quickstep*, and *Roseland fox-trot*; even dances such as the *Lindy* and the *hustle* are derived to some extent from the fox-trot.

THE PEABODY

Soon after the introduction of the fox-trot, two variations developed: a slow fox-trot done at about forty measures per minute and a fast fox-trot done at over fifty measures per minute. This was particularly apparent in England, where a convention of the Imperial Society of Teachers of Dancing in 1924 accepted the name *quickstep* to define a fast fox-trot done at fifty-four to fifty-six measures per minute. One of the basic figures was a *cross-step* (described in England as early as 1920), in which the man crossed his right foot behind his left while the woman crossed her left foot in front of her right.

In the United States, the fast fox-trot was named the *Peabody* after a Brooklyn police lieutenant* who was popular in dancing circles. It is a fast dance, characterized by rapid progression and frequent use of Right Outside Position. The basic step is the cross-step as developed in 1920.

JAZZ

After the end of the first world war, the United States witnessed a social revolution. Customs and values of previous generations were rejected; life was to be lived and enjoyed to the full. This was the era of the "lost generation," of the "sheik" with his hip flask, and the "flapper" with her rolled stockings, short skirts, and straight up-and-down look. They met and scandalized their elders in the cabarets, night clubs, and speakeasies that replaced the ballrooms of pre-war days. Relations between the sexes became freer and easier. Dancing was more informal with a close embrace and a frequent change of partner now socially acceptable.

For this generation there was only one kind of music — jazz, the perfect vehicle for dancing the fox-trot, *shimmy, rag, Charleston, black bottom*, and other steps of the period. Jazz music originated at the close of the nineteenth century in the seamy dance halls and brothels of the South and Midwest, where the word *jazz* commonly referred to sexual intercourse, and where southern blacks, delivered from slavery only a few decades before, started playing European music with Afro modifications. Though it is commonly believed that New Orleans was the birthplace of jazz, this is

---

* Lieutenant (later Captain) William Frank Peabody was a controversial member of the New York police force for many years. In 1907 he was involved in questionable activities connected with the famous Gould divorce from former actress Katherine Clemmons. On several occasions Peabody faced charges, and he was twice dismissed from the force. However, the courts upheld his contention that the underworld had framed him. At the time of his retirement in 1923, he was in charge of the 77th Precinct in Brooklyn. He never married and he died August 5, 1939, at the age of sixty-six.

not strictly true since similar styles of playing evolved in St. Louis, Memphis, Kansas City, and elsewhere. But New Orleans was and remains an important jazz center. Its wide mix of peoples and races, including the colorful international characters who gravitate to the bars and brothels of an important seaport, was a major factor in the development of jazz. The city had been under Spanish and French rule prior to the Louisiana Purchase; by 1900 it was a blend of French, Spanish, English, German, Italian, and Slavic peoples, plus the countless blacks originally brought in as slaves. Practically all the early jazz musicians came from New Orleans, and even as late as 1930 over half the important jazz musicians still called New Orleans their home town.

The first jazz bands contained a "rhythm section" consisting of a string bass, drums, and a guitar or banjo, and a "melodic section" with one or two cornets, a trombone, a clarinet, and sometimes even a violin. In later years, jazz was taken over by the large orchestras; a "society jazz band" contained fifteen or more musicians. Even today, there is a renewed interest in the "big band" era, even though this music has little to do with real jazz.

True jazz is characterized by certain essential features. The first is a tendency to stress the weak beats of the bar (second and fourth) in contrast to traditional music which stressed the first and third beats. The second feature of jazz is syncopation through an extensive repetition of short and strongly rhythmic phrases or "riffs." Syncopation was also characteristic of ragtime, but ragtime was largely limited to the piano, whereas jazz could encompass several instruments or an entire orchestra.

Another feature of genuine jazz is *swing*, a word that is almost impossible to define. Essentially, it refers to a regular but subtle pulsation which animates 4/4 time and must be present in every good jazz performance. As that famous Duke Ellington number says, "It Don't Mean a Thing if It Ain't Got that Swing," Swing cannot be written into the music and is often dependent on the interaction between the orchestra and the dancers (any band leader will tell you how the dancers can affect playing style).

In the 1930s, society orchestras capitalized on the growing interest in swing music. Benny Goodman's band, for example, was launched with tremendous publicity and its leader dubbed the "King of Swing." The growing popularity of the *Lindy* at this time also contributed to wider appreciation of swing by conventional dance bands.

THE LARGE DANCE STUDIOS

For hundreds of years it was generally believed that dancing could only be learned correctly from instruction by suitable dance masters or "professors of dancing" who wielded considerable power in the dance world. Dance teachers would meet periodically at their conventions and decree solemnly that the new dance for the coming season would be, say, the *military dip* or the *Lindbergh wave waltz* — only to find when they returned home that the public would pay no attention to their decrees. In fact, one teacher complained sadly that fashion designers seemed to be able to set new styles for women's clothing, but dance teachers seemed to have no effect on dancing styles.

Of course, there has always been some attempt to commercialize dance instruction. In 1885, for example, the annual convention of the American Society of Professors of Dancing in New York City's Grand Union Hotel held a demonstration of a new dance, the *college polka*.

"I don't like the slide," remarked S. Asher of Philadelphia.

"No," agreed Mr. Spink of Providence reflectively, "but it sells; there's no doubt of that!"

There have also been attempts to make dancing available without the presence of an instructor. Even in the nineteenth century, there were books such as *Dancing without a Master*, complete with instructions and simple foot diagrams. In 1913 in Peoria, Illinois, The National School of Dancing for Home Instruction was established by Julian Karl. And in 1918 Max Rothkugel of New York City published *Dancing Charts for Home Instruction* with foot diagrams tied to individual notes of the musical score. But all this was nothing in comparison to the event that rocked the establishment in 1920 when a new young dance teacher offered home instruction with an advertisement entitled, "How I became popular overnight!" The ad went on to say:

> Girls used to avoid me when I asked for a dance. Even the poorest dancers preferred to sit against the wall rather than dance with me. But I didn't wake up until a partner left me standing alone in the middle of the floor. That night I went home feeling pretty lonesome and mighty blue. As a social success, I was a first-class failure.

If the reader would clip the handy coupon and send for a free dance lesson, he could immediately become a popular dance partner.

The name of this revolutionary dance teacher was, of course, Arthur Murray, and eventually some five million people wrote in for his home dance lessons. This was too much for the established dance teachers. In August of 1923 the International Association of Masters of Dancing stated that, "Arthur Murray, who has established a dancing association to give instruction by mail, has no connection with our organization." At the same time, the group approved a new waltz and fox-trot, pledged a continued fight against jazz and other "unseemly" dancing, and voted an unceasing war on "so-called dancing instructors who claim to be able to teach the art of dancing through the mails."

This controversial young man was born in New York in 1895; his real name was Murray Teichman, but he later adopted the professional name

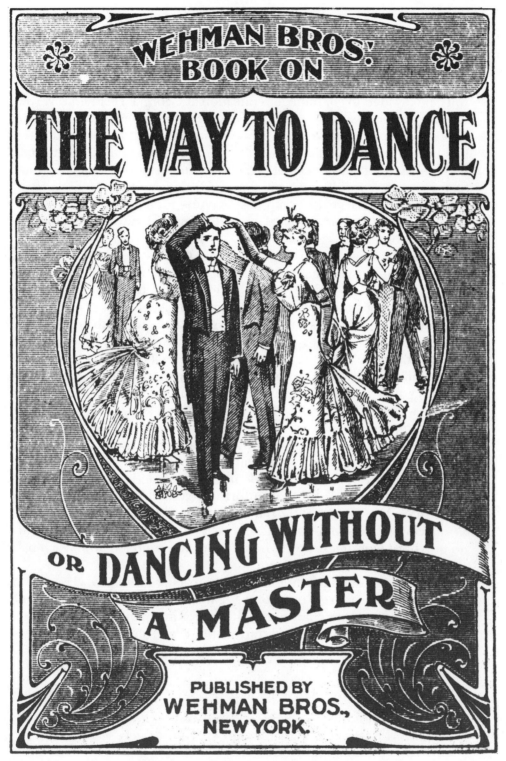

One of the first do-it-yourself dance books, circa 1898.

of Arthur Murray. He first turned to dancing as a means of meeting girls, but his commercial instincts were aroused when he won a waltz contest in 1912 at the age of seventeen. That same year he invested two hundred dollars in dance lessons from Vernon and Irene Castle, and shortly afterward he became a successful dance teacher. In 1919, at the age of twenty-four, he decided to continue his education at Georgia Tech; however, his love for dancing was too great, and he was soon involved in his mail-order dance lessons. A few years later, in 1925, he returned to New York, where he opened a studio on Forty-third Street. Thirty years later, the business had grown to become a chain of franchised studios throughout the United States.

Growth of the large dance studios revolutionized the teaching of dancing. Spending tremendous sums on advertising, they attracted millions of students from all walks of life. This unrestricted growth produced problems, and the large studios have in recent years come under increasing pressure from government agencies because of alleged high-pressure salesmanship, "bait and switch" techniques, and the use of long-term contracts. In 1960 the government ordered the Arthur Murray studios to stop using bogus contests and high-pressure tactics to sell their courses of dance instruction. In 1962 the California Office of the Attorney General began a statewide effort to stamp out a dancing school racket that reaped "many millions of dollars" from gullible persons. In 1976 Governor Carey of New York State signed a bill providing customers with safeguards in dealing with dancing schools. It is no longer necessary to sign a contract before sampling the instruction, and cancellation fees will be proportional to the services used or completed. Evidently some customers had signed "lifetime" contracts requiring an initial payment of $12,000 or more!

It should be emphasized that the number of unethical dance teachers has always been very small. It is unfortunate that this damaging publicity caused a sizable segment of the public to assume a negative attitude toward *all* dancing schools and dance teachers. Today most dance teachers are honest, hard-working people, often holding a second job, who teach ballroom dancing because they enjoy it.

There are many independent dancing teachers who give classes on a "pay-as-you-go" basis. Non-profit organizations, church groups, and municipal recreation departments often offer inexpensive group lessons. Many of the major colleges and universities, and even some high schools, are also turning back to ballroom dancing.

FRED ASTAIRE AND GINGER ROGERS

Broadway musical shows have always played an important part in the growth of ballroom dancing, although only a relatively small number of people were able to view them. The appearance of sound movies in the late 1920s made it possible for every small town to see and hear the latest shows and songs. In 1933 the movie *42nd Street* was a big hit and sparked a series of musicals starring Bing Crosby, Alice Faye, Dick Powell, Ruby Keeler, Sonja Henie, Dorothy Lamour, and many others. Hollywood attracted the best songwriters and composers such as Irving Berlin, Cole Porter, Jerome Kern, George Gershwin, Vincent Youmans, Richard Rodgers, and Lorenz Hart.

Interest in dancing was given a major boost in the 1930s by the musical comedies featuring Fred Astaire and Ginger Rogers. Fred Astaire and his sister Adele were considered an "important child act" in vaudeville as early as 1906, when Fred was seven years old. They continued in vaudeville for the next ten years, moving from town to town with their mother, often for one- or two-night stands. Eventually they tired of this life, and in 1917, were ready to try their luck in New York on the musical comedy stage. Their first show, *Over the Top*, was a modest success and was followed by nine other successful musicals during the next fifteen years, both in New York and London. In 1932 Adele retired to marry Lord Charles Cavendish, second son of the Duke of Devonshire and one of the wealthiest men in England; in 1933 Fred Astaire was married to Phyllis Potter of Long Island and signed a contract with RKO to make movies in Hollywood.

Fred first appeared in a movie called *Dancing Lady* which featured Joan Crawford and Clark Gable; his part was relatively small, but he had the advantage of appearing under his own name and it was an introduction to Hollywood. His second motion picture, in 1933, was *Flying Down to Rio* which included such song hits as "Orchids in the Moonlight" (a tango) and "The Carioca" (a samba) by Vincent Youmans. It also marked the beginning of the Fred Astaire/Ginger Rogers collaboration. *Flying Down to Rio* opened at Radio City Music Hall in New York; the nationwide release of the film shortly after its opening firmly established the dance team of Astaire and Rogers in the public eye. The following years produced *The Gay Divorcee* (with Cole Porter's "Night and Day" and "The Continental"), *Roberta* ("Smoke Gets in Your Eyes"), *Top Hat* ("Dancing Cheek to Cheek"), *Swing Time*, *Follow the Fleet*, and *The Story of Vernon and Irene Castle*.

The popularity of Astaire and Rogers movies did much to promote dancing in the days before the second world war, particularly among college students. The dance studios also profited from the Hollywood publicity, although there was never a serious attempt to convince people that dances such as the *Carioca* and the *Continental* were suited to the ballroom. In 1936 it was estimated by Donald Grant, then president of the Dancing Teachers' Business Association, that six million people were learning to dance, "many influenced by recent motion pictures which have featured dancing."

THE LINDY

In August 1927 a large group of dance instructors met in New York and agreed that popular new dances for the 1927-28 season would include the *kinkajou*, the *Yankee prance*, and the *Lindbergh wave waltz*. If these instructors had taken a ten-minute taxi ride to Harlem, they would have seen the real dance of the future!

On March 12, 1926, the Savoy Ballroom had opened at Lenox Avenue and 140th Street in New York, and as its first act featured Fletcher Henderson's band, the leading black band of the day. With a block-long dance floor and a raised double bandstand, the Savoy was an immediate success. Nightly dancing attracted most of the best dancers in the New York area, including many outstanding black dancers. By the time the Savoy closed thirty-two years later, every well-known band in the country — both black and white — had played there.

Stimulated by the presence of great dancers and the best black bands, music at the Savoy was largely swinging jazz. The dancers developed a very acrobatic style, each trying to think up new steps to outdo the others. One evening in 1927, following Lindbergh's flight to Paris, a local dance enthusiast named "Shorty George" Snowden was watching some of the more acrobatic couples and muttered, "Look at them kids hoppin' over there. I guess they're doin' the Lindy hop." Today, more than fifty years later, the *Lindy* is still one of the most popular of ballroom dances.

Although it is possible that this version of the origin of the Lindy may be fiction, it is a fact that the Lindy did originate in the Savoy Ballroom in about 1927, where it was done to swing music. The basic step was a syncopated two-step or box step that accented the offbeat; this was followed by a breakaway, the characteristic feature of the dance. Of course, the steps of the Lindy were not entirely new, since similar movements had been used in dances such as the *shag* and *Texas tommy* and in vaudeville dancing. The real contribution of the Lindy was to combine these movements on a ballroom dance floor.

Initial reaction to the Lindy was limited pretty much to Harlem and the Savoy devotees. By the end of 1936, however, the Lindy (also called *jitterbug, jive*, and *swing*) was sweeping the United States. In 1939 Duke Ellington and Paul Whiteman alternated at the first annual convention and jam session of the National Swing Club of America, held at the New York Hippodrome and attended by three thousand "swingers."

As might be expected, the first reaction of most dancing teachers to the Lindy was a chilly negative. In 1936 Philip Nutl, president of the American Society of Teachers of Dancing, expressed the opinion that swing would not last beyond the winter. In 1938 Donald Grant, president of the Dance Teachers' Business Association, said that swing music ". . . is a degenerated form of jazz, whose devotees are the unfortunate victims of economic instability." Opposition was in vain, however, and in 1942 members of the New York Society of Teachers of Dancing were told that the jitterbug, a direct descendent of the Lindy hop, could no longer be ignored. Its "cavortings" could be refined to suit a crowded dance floor.

Jitterbug enjoyed tremendous popularity from 1936 through the war years. Practically every soda "shoppe" installed a juke box so that high school students could jitterbug after school. Its popularity began to fade with the end of the war, and only recently has a modified Lindy been making a comeback — this time largely with college students.

THE RUMBA

Rumba music in more or less its present form has existed in Cuba for over a hundred years. The word *rumba* is a generic term for a type of West Indian music or dancing. The exact meaning varies from island to island. For example, in Jamaica and Haiti, the "rumba box" is a primitive musical instrument used by native musicians. In Cuba, *rumba* describes a non-religious "good time" dance of the peasants. The true rumba is of African origin and has been largely limited to the lowest strata of society because of the licentious character of the dance. The native rumba folk dance is essentially a sex pantomime danced extremely fast with exaggerated hip movements and with a sensually aggressive attitude on the part of the man and a defensive attitude on the part of the woman. Many of its figures depict simple farm tasks such as shoeing a mare, climbing a rope, or courtship in the barnyard. The music is played with a staccato beat in keeping with the vigorous expressive movements of the dancers. Primitive accompanying instruments include the *maracas*, gourds containing dried seeds or pebbles; the *claves*, two sticks which are struck together; the *marimbola* or rumba box, and the drums.

As recently as the second world war, the *son* was the popular dance of middle class Cuba. It is a modified, slower and more refined version of the native rumba with essentially the same 2/4 rhythm. The spirit of the dance is in the *claves*, which set the tempo of the music. Still slower is the *danzón*, the dance of wealthy Cuban society. The music of the *danzón* is played in two parts — a verse and a chorus. People dance only to the chorus, stopping to fan themselves while the verse is played. Very small steps are taken, with the women producing a very subtle tilting of the hips by alternately bending and straightening the knees.

The American rumba is a modified version of the *son*. The first serious attempt to introduce the rumba to the United States was by Lew Quinn and Joan Sawyer in 1913. Ten years later band leader Emil Coleman imported some rumba musicians and a pair of rumba dancers to New York, but no interest in the dance developed at that time. In 1925 Benito Collada opened the Club El Chico in Greenwich Village and found that New

Yorkers did not know what the rumba was all about. Customers tried it and suggested he hire an Irish tenor! A black checkroom attendant is credited with saving him from bankruptcy in 1927 by doing the *Charleston* nightly to great applause.

Real interest in Latin music began about 1929 as a result of increased American tourism to Latin America. In the summer of 1930 the Edward Marks Music Company published "The Peanut Vender," and America suddenly became aware of Latin-American music as a source of dance numbers. In the late 1920s Xavier Cugat formed an orchestra that specialized in Latin-American music. He opened at the Cocoanut Grove in Los Angeles and appeared in early sound movies such as *In Gay Madrid*, starring Ramon Novarro in 1930. Later in the 1930s, Cugat played at the Waldorf-Astoria Hotel in New York and by the end of the decade was recognized as having the outstanding Latin orchestra of the day. In 1935 George Raft played the part of a suave dancer in the movie *Rumba*, a rather superficial musical in which the hero finally won the heiress (Carole Lombard) through their mutual love of dancing.

The American rumba is done in a box pattern similar to the waltz but with much smaller steps. Its chief characteristic is "Cuban motion," a discreet but expressive hip movement achieved by carefully timed weight transfer. English rumba is done with forward-and-back steps as in the Cuban style. Although some Latin-Americans appear to resent the United States version — which they feel spoils the dance — American rumba seems to be here to stay and remains one of the most popular of our ballroom dances.

THE SAMBA

Two Brazilian folk dances have made their way to the American ballroom, the *maxixe* and the *samba*. Starting about 1910 the *maxixe*, or *tango Brésilien*, was popular in this country for about ten years. It was favored by society dance teachers such as the Castles, who included the *maxixe* as one of the few dances that received their stamp of approval. It was not an easy dance to learn, however, and never obtained wide acceptance by the general dancing public. It is still danced to some extent in northern Brazil.

The ballroom samba or *carioca* samba is derived from the rural "rocking samba" and has been known for many years. (The Carioca is a small river that runs through Rio de Janiero — hence the name *carioca* refers to the people of Rio.) The samba in its primitive form was introduced to the city by the blacks who came downtown on holidays or at carnival time. About 1917 the ballroom version was born. Much of samba music came from daily life in Rio, the first famous example being "Pelo Telefone" composed by Donga. Today samba is still very popular in Rio. During carnival time there are "schools of samba" involving thousands of elaborately-costumed dancers presenting a national theme based on music typical of Brazil and Rio in particular.

As early as 1923 an international meeting of professors of dancing took note of the rise of the samba's popularity, particularly in France. A French dance book published by Paul Boucher in 1928 included samba instructions. The dance was introduced to United States movie audiences in 1933 when Fred Astaire and Dolores Del Rio danced the carioca in *Flying Down to Rio* and several years later, Carmen Miranda danced the samba in *That Night in Rio*. A samba exhibition was given at the November 1938 meeting of the New York Society of Teachers of Dancing. General interest in the samba was stimulated at the 1939 World's Fair in New York, where samba music was played at the Brazilian Pavilion. A few years later the Brazilian composer Ary Barroso wrote the classic samba, "Brasil," which quickly became a hit, and in 1944 he went to Hollywood to write the score for the musical *Brazil*.

The samba is now a moderately popular ballroom dance, limited pretty much to advanced ballroom dancers because of its speed and difficulty. Principal characteristics of the samba are the rapid "cuts" or steps taken on a quarter of a beat and the pronounced rocking motion and sway of the dancing couple.

THE MERENGUE

There are two popular versions (both fictional) of the origin of the Dominican national dance, the *merengue*. One story alleges the dance originated with slaves who were chained together and, of necessity, were forced to drag one leg as they cut sugar to the beat of drums. The second alleges that a great hero was wounded in the leg during one of the many revolutions in the Dominican Republic. A party of villagers welcomed him home with a victory celebration and, out of sympathy, everyone dancing felt obliged to limp and drag one foot.

The facts are that the merengue has existed since the early years of the Dominican Republic (in Haiti, a similar dance is called the *meringue*). It is possible the dance took its name from the confection made of sugar and egg whites — because of the light and frothy character of the dance or because of its short, precise rhythms. By the middle of the nineteenth century, it was very popular in the Dominican Republic.

As in the case of all Latin-American dances, the native version is fast and agitated. The ballroom merengue is slower and has a modified hip action. It is probably the easiest Latin dance to learn and is essentially a "fun" dance. Characteristics of the dance include a basic chassé with Cuban Motion, small steps, and no movement above the waist. Although the merengue was introduced in the United States about 1950 it did not become well known in the New York area until several years later. Now a favorite with advanced dancers across the country, it is surprising — in view of its simplicity and enjoyable nature — that the merengue has not received wider recognition from the dancing public.

THE MAMBO

In the back country of Haiti, the *mambo* is a voodoo priestess who serves the villagers as counselor, healer, exorcist, soothsayer, spiritual adviser, and organizer of public entertainment. Although she is often associated with voodoo music and ritual dancing, there is no folk dance in Haiti called the "mambo." A mambo dance originated in Cuba, however, where there are substantial settlements of Haitians, and it is entirely possible that there was some voodoo influence behind the name.

The mambo dance as we know it is attributed to Perez Prado, who introduced it at La Tropicana nightclub in Havana in 1943. It was brought over to the United States soon after, but did not achieve popularity overnight. Its first congenial home was in New York's Park Plaza Ballroom at Fifth Avenue and 110th Street, a favorite hangout of enthusiastic dancers from Harlem. Soon fair-skinned dance teachers from the fashionable studios were coming to watch this new dance, first out of curiosity and later because of its commercial possibilities. Enthusiasm for the rumba was on the wane by the late 1940s, and the mambo was seen as an opportunity to recapture the imaginations (and bankrolls) of former rumba students and to attract new thousands at the same time.

The first challenge was to modify the dance by toning down the more violent acrobatics. A ballroom mambo was then presented to the public at dance studios, resort hotels, and at nightclubs in New York and Miami. The result was an artistic and commercial success. Smiling dance teachers were soon working eight hours a day turning out mambo-happy dancers, known affectionately as "mambonicks." Magazine articles appeared with titles such as "Uncle Sambo — Mad for Mambo." Rosemary Clooney sang "Mambo Italiano," and Nat King Cole sang "Papa Loves Mambo." There were even songs such as "I Saw Mommy Do the Mambo (with you know who)" and a tear-jerker entitled "They Were Doin' the Mambo" about a boy who lost his girl to a friend who could do the mambo.

In England, where both rumba and mambo are danced with a forward-and-back basic step to a *quick-quick-slow* rhythm, the mambo is considered to be merely a modification of the rumba. In the United States, where the box-style rumba basic is most widely used, dance teachers regard the mambo as a dance quite separate from the rumba.

The mambo dance craze did not last long, and today mambo is pretty much limited to advanced dancers. It is fairly fast with a jerky staccato effect. Possibly the greatest contribution of the mambo is the fact that it led to development of the cha-cha.

THE CHA-CHA

In the islands of the West Indies, there are certain plants that produce seed pods called *cha-cha* or (depending on the island) *tcha-tcha* or *kwa-kwa*. These are used to make a small rattle also known as a *cha-cha*. In Haiti, the typical voodoo band consists of three drums, a bell, and a *cha-cha*. The *cha-cha* is used by the leader as a guide instrument or "metronome" to set the time in secular dancing as well as in religious music and singing.

Even during the popularity peak of the mambo, many dancers did not care for it because, they claimed, it seemed to go against the natural rhythm of the music. In particular, many ballroom dancers criticized the fast mambos for having the acrobatic character of jitterbug rather than the smooth movements usually associated with Latin dance. In 1953 the Cuban orchestra América started playing the time-honored *danzón* with a new syncopated beat. This sounded like a very slow mambo, and Cuban dancers used a slight triple hip undulation on the slow count. Gradually this was changed to a triple step on the slow count, and the *cha-cha* was born. The cha-cha was introduced to the United States in 1954, and by 1959 Americans were "ga-ga over cha-cha," with dance studios reporting it to be their most popular dance.

Most ballroom dancers are much more comfortable with cha-cha rhythm than with mambo rhythm, and it lends itself easily to many variations from the basic steps. Today, twenty-five years after its creation, the cha-cha remains the most popular Latin dance in the United States.

THE BOSSA NOVA

The most recently introduced Latin dance is the *bossa nova*, a smooth fusion of the Brazilian samba *canção* with American jazz. (In Brazil, *bossa nova* is a slang expression that can be loosely translated as "the new beat.") Bossa nova music was heard in the cafes of Rio starting about 1958. Its evolution is attributed largely to three talented young Brazilians, singer-guitarist-composer Joao Gilberto, composer-arranger-conductor Antonio Carlos Jobim (who wrote "Desafinado"), and guitarist Louis Bonfa. Jobim and Bonfa collaborated on the musical score for the film *Black Orpheus*. Later such songs as "The Girl from Ipanema" and "Blame It on the Bossa Nova" did much to publicize bossa nova music. Credit should also be given to Sidney Frey, president of Audio Fidelity Records and a Brazilian by birth, who helped bring the music to the United States and who sponsored a bossa nova festival at Carnegie Hall. Many of the musical themes for the bossa nova came from love songs, costumes, and daily life of the people of Rio.

The bossa nova dance originated about 1960 and achieved moderate popularity by 1962. The dance is done to a *slow-quick-quick* rhythm, in contrast to the *quick-quick-slow* of the American rumba. It is probably safe to say that the bossa nova dance has never been as popular as its music, which is surprising since the dance is easy to learn and has many interesting figures.

THE BIG BAND ERA

The popularity of jazz and swing in the 1930s led to imitation by predominantly white musicians who created a new musical vehicle — the big band. Early jazz bands such as Fletcher Henderson's, Louis Armstrong's, and Duke Ellington's were basically rhythm or swing bands. They played in ballrooms, nightclubs, and cabarets where the primary interest was dancing. The typical jazz band contained eleven musicians with three trumpets, one trombone, three reeds, and four rhythms.

The typical big band, on the other hand, included four trumpets, three or four trombones, five reeds, and four rhythms. Paul Whiteman's orchestra, a popular society dance band of the early 1930s, also included strings and other instruments inimical to swing.

One of the early big bands was led by Benny Goodman, the "King of Swing," who played "streamlined jazz." When he played at the Paramount Theater in New York in 1936, high school kids began jitterbugging in the aisles. The Fire Department was called in to check the safety of the balcony, and the following day's newspaper headlines from coast to coast announced the arrival of the swing era.

Other big bands came along — led by Guy Lombardo, Tommy and Jimmy Dorsey, Glenn Miller, Artie Shaw, Woody Herman, Gene Krupa, Jimmy Lunceford, and Harry James, to name a few. Their audiences would come to jitterbug, to dance to slow or fast fox-trots, or just to listen. By 1940 a trend was starting toward the use of concert halls — which were, of course, much more profitable since there was no need to provide space for dancing and the seating capacity was thus much greater. This, in turn, led to a gradual change in the music, with less swing and more "concert" music for easy listening. Slow numbers were introduced, and the big band of 1940 showed little resemblance to the black jazz band of 1930.

The period from 1942 to 1945 was disastrous for the big bands. Recording bans, the federal tax on dance floors, increased costs, and the new styles of music all took their toll. The second world war produced blackouts, rationing of food and gasoline, and the draft with its shortage of men. By

1945 ballrooms were folding and big bands were breaking up. Orchestras such as Guy Lombardo's managed to survive intact by playing "sweet" or "society" music (known in the trade as "the businessman's bounce").

Now, more than thirty years later, there is a renewed interest in big bands. Based primarily on nostalgia, several of the big bands have been recreated under their old names and have been making successful tours of colleges, schools, and concert halls throughout the United States. This is undoubtedly related to the renewed interest in ballroom dancing, and much of today's "big band" enthusiasm probably results from a desire for more melodious and danceable music rather than from a sentimental interest in the big bands *per se*. However, with the rapid advances in electronic amplification, a much smaller group of musicians can produce an equally satisfactory effect so that the big band is completely unnecessary for today's ballroom dancing.

THE INFLUENCE OF RADIO AND TELEVISION

Radio became available to the general public in 1922, and the first nationwide networks were formed a few years later. By the early 1930s radio was making a substantial impact on the American way of life, and stars such as Jack Benny, Will Rogers, Kate Smith, Bing Crosby, and Amos 'n' Andy were known throughout the nation. Early radio bands included those of Paul Whiteman, Rudy Vallee, Guy Lombardo, Fred Waring, and Wayne King. These bands played "sweet" music, since the general public outside major urban centers at that time did not care for jazz. Listening to the radio was still a family affair, and it would still be several years before the typical teenager or college student could have a radio for his personal enjoyment.

Early radio was probably helpful for dancing since the first bands on the air were dance bands. During the 1930s, practically every large hotel in New York had a dance orchestra, and many of these were heard on the radio. Thus, when Fred Waring and his Pennsylvanians were on the air, everyone knew that people were dancing to his music in the ballroom of the Hotel Pennsylvania. Each week the radio "Hit Parade" played the most popular tunes of the day, most of them dance numbers. "Make Believe Ballroom" was another program widely listened to — and danced to — by young people.

The close of the second world war in 1945 witnessed a complete change in the listening habits of the radio audience. Small portable radios became available. Instead of family listening, most of the programs now became oriented to the teenager and college student, whose hero was the disc jockey. New styles of music were introduced, using more vocalists and novelty tunes, and smaller bands experimented with unusual sound effects. Singers such as Frank Sinatra and Peggy Lee were the idols of the day. In 1955, when rock-and-roll began to take over, amplifiers were turned up and the homes of teenagers literally shook to the sound of a rocking jazz combo with its honking tenor sax and big offbeat. Elvis Presley and The Beatles appeared on the scene. As far as radio was concerned, ballroom dancing was dead.

The end of the war also witnessed the appearance of a new electronic force — television. By the early 1950s, watching television was becoming the chief "spectator sport" in the United States. Nobody could find time to dance if it meant missing a favorite program! Even the few dance programs on TV were of little help. Dick Clark's "American Bandstand" featured "bop," a watered-down and rather dismal form of the Lindy which was successful only in discouraging interest in dancing on the part of the new generation of teenagers. Arthur Murray and his wife Kathryn Murray produced a program in which members of the studio audience were taught a few dance steps; home viewers were encouraged to try the steps and, of course, if they had any problems, to drop in at the nearest Arthur Murray studio for a little help. The Murrays also sponsored a celebrity dance contest on TV, but these efforts did not bring about a renewed interest in ballroom dancing on the part of the TV-watching public.

Lawrence Welk's orchestra became a standard weekly program on TV in the early 1960s. As far as the young people were concerned, this was not for them. They associated it primarily with the older generation who were seen dancing on the program and for whom the commercials were clearly designed. As far as ballroom dancing is concerned, TV remains pretty much a wasteland today. An occasional polka party, shots of dancers in early movies, and novelty and jazz dance programs — together with the continued success of Lawrence Welk — just about sums it up.

ROCK-AND-ROLL

Originally a black expression with sexual connotations, the term *rock-and-roll* was well known to black musicians and vaudeville artists for many years before it became the darling of the disk jockeys. Its first introduction to the general public was in a 1934 motion picture called *Transatlantic Merry-Go-Round* featuring Jack Benny. At that time, the Boswell Sisters introduced the song "Rock and Roll" with music by Richard Whiting and lyrics by Sidney Clare, and it became one of the most popular songs of the year. In 1937 a song entitled "Rock It for Me," with music and lyrics by Kay and Sue Werner, was recorded by several orchestras, including Chick Webb and Jimmy Lunceford, The lyrics began "Came to town with a new kind of rhythm . . ." and ended with ". . . won't you satisfy your soul with a rock and roll."

In 1954 a mid-western disk jockey named Alan Freed moved to radio station WINS in New York City. His "Rock 'n Roll Party" combined blues, rhythm, and hill-billy music and soon became the biggest thing in radio. In 1954 Bill Haley and the Comets recorded "Shake, Rattle, and Roll," and in 1955 their "Rock Around the Clock" was the top record of the year, with sales of over three million copies. Elvis Presley and other singers appeared on the scene, and soon rock numbers created the phenomenon known as the "Top Forty," which has dominated the field of popular music ever since.

The tremendous growth of interest in rock was dependent largely on teenagers with portable transister radios. Many of these children of the second world war felt themselves an alien group in an unfriendly adult world. They identified with the disk jockeys and with their new form of distraction and escape. Unlike many previous alienated teenagers, this generation had buying power and could back up its demands. From 1956 on there was a succession of songs written for them, such as "Teen Age Crush," "Ballad of a Teenage Queen," "All Shook Up," "A White Shirt, Coat, and a Pink Carnation," and so on.

This early and uncomplicated form of rock was essentially "fun" music for "fun" dancing. By 1961, however, rock, now entering its revolutionary period, had developed the most kinetic beat since the invention of tom-toms. In San Francisco, starting about 1965, "acid rock," or music that attempted to reproduce the sense disorientation of a person under the influence of LSD, was gaining popularity among a generation experimenting with drugs. Another strain of rock known as "head music" tried to enhance the marijuana experience.

THE TWIST

With the advent of rock-and-roll music in the early 1960s, another dance fad swept through the United States : the *twist*. Based partly on an earlier dance called *The Madison*, the twist was described as ". . . a shoulder-shaking, hip-swiveling step in which partners synchronize their movements but do not touch." In 1955 Hank Ballard had recorded a song called "The Twist." Its fame was spread by Chubby Checker, a singer with a small combo, who plugged the song and the new dance across the country. In New York, the Peppermint Lounge became informal headquarters for twist dancers who swayed and rocked to such numbers as "The Twist," "You Can't Sit Down," "Fanny May," and "The Peppermint Twist."

Toward the end of 1961, Cafe Society, which had so far rejected rock music, suddenly accepted the twist. When the Metropolitan Museum of Art in New York City held a reception, director James Rorimer was dismayed to see hundreds of guests swaying to the new dance. Many of them urged the band to continue even if it delayed the rest of the program.

In Washington, a spokesman for the White House firmly denied that President Kennedy or anyone else had danced the twist at a recent party there. Lou Brecker, founder of Roseland Dance City in New York, announced that the twist would be banned in Roseland. "It is lacking in true grace and, since we have previously outlawed rock-and-roll, we likewise will not permit the twist to be danced." Motion pictures capitalized on the new dance craze with titles such as *Twist Around the Clock* and *Hey, Let's Twist*. Enthusiasm for the twist, however, faded within a year or two, although its music is still played occasionally for those who remember the lively beat and enjoy its gyrations.

DISCO

In France, private clubs found that they did not need live musicians to get people to dance — a *disquaire* to program dance records and moods for the evening worked just as well, if not better. Such a place soon had a name: *discothèque* (record library). The first Parisian discothèque, called *Whiskey à Go-Go*, opened in the late 1940s; when the first discothèque, called simply *Le Club*, opened in New York, it was a raging success. Dozens and then thousands of discothèques opened across the nation in a new dance craze that continues to the present. By 1965 there were over five thousand discothèques in the United State alone. Many of these stuck to the original formula of using only recorded music, often to the accompaniment of colored or strobe lighting for an enhanced effect of unreality. Others use live bands, and many of today's best known rock groups got their start in discothèques.

Rock-and-roll has almost represented a death blow to ballroom dancing for a number of reasons. There is no need to take lessons or learn how to dance rock — everyone simply does his or her "own thing." Rock bands are small, often made up of musicians who do not read music. Their effect is based largely on electronic amplification, which is the only real expense involved, and the audiences are not highly critical. Large dance floors are unnecessary. Catering to young people with money in their pockets, most lounges and many restaurants were easily converted to rock. By 1970 ballroom dancing was once again at a very low ebb.

THE REVIVAL OF BALLROOM DANCING

The story behind the present renewed interest in ballroom dancing is told very well by R.J. Stupak in an article in *The Christian Century* entitled "Return to the Ballroom: They Shoot Students, Don't They?" When the shots rang out at Kent State University in May of 1970, the mood on college and university campuses changed abruptly. Kent State was not the entire cause of this change, but it literally dealt the final blow to the excitement and headiness of the "demonstration decade" of the 1960s. "The System kills" became stark reality, not only to serious radical students but — more tellingly — to the marginal hangers-on who had flitted around the edges of the incessant meetings, rock concerts, and rap sessions more for the excitement than from deep commitment to any revolutionary or ideological causes. It became evident that a college campus would no longer be tolerated as a protected community apart from the rest of the American political system. From that moment the activist community was effectively fractured both as a practical reality and as an ideal.

Suddenly in the 1970s college campuses have become places of non-involvement and political apathy. Conservatism of all kinds, accompanied by renewed interest in athletics, fraternities and sororities, and in such things as frisbee contests, streaking, and beer blasts, is "in." Enrollment in practical subjects such as engineering and business has mushroomed at the expense of the humanities. Nowhere has the transformation been more noticeable than in the growing enthusiasm of college students for ballroom dancing.

Dancing in the 1960s had reflected the mood of the students. Their confidence in themselves, their independence, and their futures was demonstrated by rock music, reckless and abandoned dancing, and their ease with continually changing partners. The uncertainties of the 1970s, however, have shown that nothing is guaranteed — teachers, lawyers, sociologists, and many other trained professionals have found suddenly that their jobs were oversolicited. Many students are filled with doubts and fears about the future — and today there is a need for someone to hold onto, someone to commiserate with. Ballroom dancing helps to fill this need for a return to couples and to a structured one-to-one relationship. The mutual effort and fun of "touch dancing" for these students reflects a trend toward more permanent and monogamous relationships and away from sexual experimentation on campus.

THE HUSTLE

The return to ballroom dancing was greatly facilitated in the early 1970s by the introduction of the *hustle*. Danced to disco music (although essentially a six-count Lindy), the dance was musically acceptable to young people and yet represented a return to close-couple dancing. Van McCoy's recording of "The Hustle" made the national charts for eighteen weeks. Articles in newspapers announced "Touch dancing is back," "They're Together Again," "People are tired of being away from the person they want to be with," and the public nodded in agreement.

The word *hustle* actually stems from the Dutch word for "shake"; in underworld lingo, a hustler was one who shook up or jostled a victim while his confederate picked his pocket. In the United States, the word has been generally applied to an aggressive go-getter, but more particularly to a hard-working prostitute. The hustle dance originated about 1970 in the black and Puerto Rican bars of the boroughs of Manhattan and Queens in New York City. Its popularity followed and blended with the disco explosion. Dance teachers were quick to recognize the commercial possibilities of the hustle, and in many studios it has been the dance most requested, especially by young people.

As this book goes to press, the many versions of hustle include *Latin hustle, Lindy hustle, American hustle, tango hustle, three-count hustle*, and *street hustle* — with some being far more difficult than others. So far the constantly changing patterns have proven somewhat frustrating for most dancers and it is obvious that the dance needs to be simplified and standardized or the public will simply reject it as being too complicated to bother with. The *American hustle*, which we describe later in this book, is the easiest version and best suited for the beginner. Whatever becomes of the hustle itself as a dance, the fact remains that is has provided a bridge back to ballroom dancing for young and old alike.

BALLROOM DANCING TODAY AND TOMORROW

The really significant feature in today's revival of ballroom dancing is the renewed interest on the part of young people. This is partly the result of demographic changes. The post-war babies have grown up and become more conservative — the "teenage culture" of the 1960s is gone. The return to the ballroom represents a symbolic revolt against the excesses of the previous years: the war in Viet Nam, environmental devastation, and the crass commercialization of our society which has made young people yearn for change. Even the artificial and highly amplified blasts of rock music are increasingly yielding to slow, easy music and country-western. Songs of the country road and of "Rocky Mountain High" can be viewed as a subconscious turning toward a safe and less-complicated world.

In 1974 the Arthur Murray studios reported a 25 per cent increase in enrollment, with a 30 per cent increase among those under thirty. There has been a rebirth of ballroom dancing at colleges and universities throughout the country. Yale University recently brought Lester Lanin, one of the old-time "society" bands, to New Haven. Vassar College in 1976 held a senior prom complete with fox-trots and dance cards. Attendance at the University of Connecticut's Monday night dance classes, now in their sixth year, continues to average over a hundred students. In August of 1977 the American Ballroom Company attracted nearly five hundred entrants from colleges throughout the country for a dance contest held at the Grand Ballroom of New York's Waldorf-Astoria Hotel.

Another indication of the renewed interest in "touch dancing" is the polka craze that has swept the country in recent years. The old Bohemian dance has been adopted as a "national dance" in this country by Polish and other ethnic groups. Encouraged by orchestras such as Lawrence Welk's, *polkaholics* follow their favorite local polka bands from club to club, often attending *polkathons* that continue for days.

There are two major problems faced by today's ballroom dancers. First, there is a real "generation gap" of people from about twenty-five to forty-five who have never been exposed to any form of dancing except rock. Most of them will never take the time or trouble to learn ballroom dancing at this point in their lives — they will rock or just not dance at all.

The second problem is economic. Ballroom dancers require a large floor and good music; they are usually moderate in their eating and drinking habits — not the favorite customers of restaurants and lounges. A rock combo costs less, occupies less space, and usually can be counted on to sell more drinks! As long as rock groups and disco continue to attract customers, there is no economic incentive to provide ballroom dancing.

If today's "return to the ballroom" by college students continues, it will eventually make an impact on the entertainment industry. The interest in ballroom dancing is already beginning to sift down to the high schools. Churches, municipal recreation departments, private clubs, and other groups are responding more and more to the demand for lessons in ballroom dancing, and there is a gradual recognition of the fact that ballroom dancing is a more wholesome activity than bending the elbow at a bar or lounge. If society does recognize and encourage this return to the ballroom, it will go a long way toward the solution of some of its problems.

II

BASIC BALLROOM SKILLS, MUSIC, AND LANGUAGE

Techniques

Before describing the individual dances, let us take a good look at some of the basic techniques used in all ballroom dancing. The beginner will find that careful attention to a few elementary principles will greatly facilitate his progress. Every dance teacher has seen pupils who have spent thousands of dollars on lessons (elsewhere, of course) and yet look awkward and uncomfortable on the dance floor. There are also those pupils who have spent relatively little on lessons and yet stand tall as they go through simple figures in a relaxed and confident way — looking like a million dollars!

About a hundred years ago, a well-known New York society dance teacher was upset when one of his new pupils asked, "How do you haul your partner around?" Even today, many men appear to feel that dance success is achieved by learning how to push and pull the woman through complicated movements. They just don't realize that force is never required on a dance floor!

Good posture and a correct and firm hold are the two most important features of good ballroom dancing. Poor posture not only gives an appearance of bad style but also seriously affects the balance and guidance of the dancers. A couple should literally move as one, striving for a smooth and relaxed motion across the floor. Until this is achieved, knowledge of more difficult figures will never make them appear as good dancers.

CLOSED POSITION

The most common position for ballroom dancing is Closed Position, with the couple facing each other about six inches apart. Both stand tall with head up, waist taut, and shoulders relaxed. The man's right hand is placed firmly on the woman's back just below her left shoulder blade, with fingers and thumb held together (not spread) and the forearm slanting downward in a straight line from elbow to fingertips. The woman rests her left arm lightly on the man's right arm with her fingers on his shoulder and her wrist on his upper arm. The woman's left arm should follow the curve of the man's right arm, and it is important to the lead that the man keep his right elbow raised sufficiently for the woman's entire forearm to make contact.

Closed Position (a)   Closed Position (b)

The man holds the woman's right hand in his left, with palm facing forward and thumbs crossed, the woman's fingers held between his thumb and index finger. This hold should be relaxed and "unfussy." The two hands are held an equal distance between the partners at about the level of the woman's ear. The man's left arm and the woman's right arm curve slightly downward from shoulder to elbow, and this part of their arms should be held well back so that the elbow extends directly to the side, not forward. It is a common mistake for the man to allow his left elbow to move forward, thereby forcing the woman's right arm backward. The man's left wrist must not bend, and there should be an unbroken line from elbow to wrist.

Even though elbows are raised, shoulders remain at normal height. It is also particularly important that the man's and woman's shoulders remain parallel to each other. Beginners often tend to push with their clasped hands, forcing their shoulders back into a "V" alignment.

A couple never dances toe to toe. The woman stands slightly to the man's right, so that on forward steps his left foot is outside of her and his right foot is pointed between her feet. Both the man and woman look over the partner's right shoulder; it is very bad form to look at the floor. In the United States, it is customary to dance six inches apart; an exception to this is the tango, which is danced with "no daylight" between the partners. In the International Style of dancing as developed in England all dances are done with this closer hold. Interestingly enough, one of the biggest problems with beginners in this country is to get them to dance close enough.

Rules of posture, of course, are a matter of individual style and hence subject to modification. Sometimes it is possible to be too precise; for example, one of Arthur Murray's pupils, an M.D., once asked, "Which vertebra do I hold?" Dance position must obviously be modified if there is a substantial difference in the height of the partners. Latin dances require a slightly different lead and hold from the fox-trot and waltz. For dances such as the polka, Lindy, and hustle, posture is relatively unimportant. Generally speaking, you and your partner will dance your best when you are most comfortable in your contact.

In ballroom dancing, the man leads and the woman follows. The most important requirement for the man is to be thoroughly familiar with the figures of a dance so that he can take his partner through them in a relaxed and confident manner. *Remember it is far better to do a few simple figures well and with style than to stumble through complicated routines.* This is particularly true with a new partner: try a few basic steps at first to determine her skill in dancing and then, if justified, try something a little more advanced.

Early ballroom dance teachers taught a stylized form of dancing similar to today's ballet. For forward steps, the feet were turned out and weight was placed first on the ball of the foot; for backward steps, the heels were never supposed to touch the floor. Even as recently as 1946, Arthur Murray was still teaching this style. Today, however, practically all dance teachers have adopted the English style, where the feet are pointed straight ahead as in walking; slow forward steps are taken with the heel hitting the floor first, while most backward steps are taken on the ball of the foot and then lowered to the heel.

LEADING

It is essential that the man signal a lead before he moves his foot. The forward lead in dancing is a "diaphragm" lead transmitted via contact between the partners. The man stands tall with his weight on the balls of his feet and inclines his upper body slightly forward to indicate the lead. He then steps toward his partner, keeping his hips and upper body directly over the supporting foot. Male beginners often are afraid of stepping on their partners' feet, so they hold back their weight and try to step outside the woman (something like a "duck walk"). It is not correct to lead with the knees, and legs must be kept together so that the man moves directly toward his partner.

Dance position requires a firm hold, so that only gentle pressure with the right hand is needed to lead a partner. The man's left hand is never used for leading except when the partners separate. When the man steps backward, he leads the woman toward him using gentle pressure on her back with his right hand. When he steps to the side, the couple will "open up" if he presses the *heel* of his right hand gently on the woman's back, and pressure of the *fingers* will return her to Closed Position. The lead for turns comes from the turning action of the body with very slight pressure of the right hand. Side steps should be directly to the side, and backward steps directly back.

In a smooth dance such as the fox-trot, knees are always kept soft so that the couple glides across the floor without marked up-and-down movement. This is achieved by bending the knees the same amount for each step. In tango, knees are flexed more than in any other dance and remain so throughout the dance. In other dances, such as the waltz and samba, there is a characteristic bending and straightening of the knees for each measure of music.

In most dances there is no motion above the hips. Shoulders remain quiet and parallel to the floor, with no bending at the waist and no bouncing up and down. Particularly unattractive is the "pump-handle" motion, where the man raises and lowers the clasped hands with each step.

Since the man must lead, he establishes the character and tempo of the dance. He listens to the music and makes sure of the timing before he begins to dance. Nothing is more frustrating to a woman than a partner who cannot keep time to the music. In the United States, it is customary to start all dances on the man's left foot (woman's right). When the music is fast, shorter steps are taken, and when it is slow, longer steps. It is a good idea, in general, for a man to dance with different partners rather than with just one who is familiar with his style of dancing. Relax, be natural, and remember that dancing is for fun!

FOLLOWING

In one respect ballroom dancing is easier for the woman. The man not only has to know what his own feet are supposed to be doing but also must lead his partner through the figures. If a woman knows the timing and a few elementary figures of a dance, she can usually relax and follow many other figures if the lead is sure and well timed. There are many women, in fact, who are excellent dancers — yet who follow steps so automatically that they are unable to show anyone else exactly what they are doing.

In another respect, however, ballroom dancing is more difficult for the woman. While the man usually travels forward in a manner little different from his natural walk, his partner usually travels backward in a manner quite different from that found in any other sport and recreation. This unfamiliar use of her muscles often makes it difficult for the beginner to achieve correct poise and balance and is a good reason for women to learn to dance at an early age.

To begin the backward walk, the woman stands tall with knees softened and body inclined very slightly backward so that some of the weight is over her heels. Weight is transferred to the left foot in readiness. Upon receiving the lead, she extends her right leg in a straight line from hip to toes and then lowers it so that weight is taken first on the ball of the foot. At this point, the heel of her left foot and the ball of her right foot will be in contact with the floor while the weight is transferred. The left foot is drawn back, and the right heel is slowly lowered to the floor — *making sure it does not touch the floor until the left foot is opposite it.* The most important features of the backward walk are keeping the weight back, extending the leg in a straight line from the hip, and the gradual lowering of the back heel. Remember that the body always moves slightly before the feet. Stretch out and enjoy these long steps, keeping the weight over the heels. If the woman presses forward or leans on her partner, it makes it difficult for him to lead and retards his forward movement.

One more word about timing. If you watch a couple dancing, you will notice that the woman always steps slightly after the man. This delay produces a slight resistance, and the resulting pressure is the most important factor in leading and following. If the woman moves exactly with her partner (and this happens when she consciously or unconsciously takes over the lead), this pressure is lost and there is no lead. *It is essential that some pressure be maintained between the partners at all times.*

POSITIONS

Although Closed Position is used most often in ballroom dancing, there are many others, and it is important to learn them well before trying to follow instructions for the individual dances. Those most often used today are:

RIGHT OUTSIDE POSITION (ROP): Right Outside Position is similar to Closed Position except that the woman is placed strongly to the man's right so that the couple's right shoulders are opposite each other. As in Closed Position, shoulders are parallel, and the woman is backing in the direction the man is facing. Forward steps by the man are taken outside the woman's right side. To go into Right Outside Position from Closed Position, both partners make an eighth turn left while maintaining their usual dance hold. The man leads by gentle pressure on the woman's back with his right hand as his body begins to turn. *Forced turning or "steering" is unnecessary.*

Right Outside Position

LEFT OUTSIDE POSITION (LOP): Left Outside Position is similar to Right Outside Position except that the woman is placed to the man's left side so that the couple's left shoulders are opposite each other. Shoulders are parallel, and the woman is backing in the direction the man is facing. Forward steps by the man are taken outside the woman's left side. It is possible to go into Left Outside Position from Closed Position merely by making an eighth turn right. More commonly, the couple first go into Right Outside Position and then turn to Left Outside Position by making a quarter turn right as the man steps forward with his right foot outside his partner.

Left Outside Position

PROMENADE POSITION: Promenade Position is often assumed in preparation for making a side step. In Promenade Position, the man's right hip and the woman's left hip are in contact or near contact, and the opposite sides of the body open out to form a "V". In some dances, such as the Lindy, the "V" is opened somewhat wider and there is no hip contact. This is sometimes referred to as *semi-open*.

Promenade Position

OPEN PROMENADE POSITION: In Open Promenade Position, the partners are about one step apart with the man holding the woman's left hand in his right with palms turned down. Partners are opened out so the bodies form a wide "V" opening to the man's left. Free arms are held at about shoulder height with palms turned down.

Open Promenade Position

COUNTER PROMENADE POSITION: This is the opposite of Promenade Position. The man's left hip and the woman's right hip are in or near contact, and the opposite sides of the body are opened into a compact "V." Since the position is rather restrictive, the man's right arm may be slightly extended to allow greater freedom of movement.

Counter Promenade Position

OPEN COUNTER PROMENADE POSITION: This is the opposite of Open Promenade Position. Here the man holds the woman's right hand in his left, and the "V" opens to the man's right. Free arms are held at shoulder height with palms down.

Open Counter Promenade Position

OPEN BREAK POSITION: Partners are about one step apart, facing each other, with the man holding the woman's right hand in his left with palms down. Free arms are held at about shoulder height with palms down.

Open Break Position

CHALLENGE POSITION: Partners are facing each other about one step apart with no contact. Arms are held at about shoulder height with palms down.

Challenge Position

CUDDLE POSITION: In Cuddle Position, the woman is at the man's right or left side, both facing in the same direction. The man has one arm across the back of his partner while the position of his other arm depends on the method of arriving in Cuddle Position. This is sometimes known as Skating Position or *Varsouvienne*.

Cuddle Position

STEPS

All dance figures are a series of steps, with each step representing a change of weight. All directions are given with reference to the supporting foot, and steps may be forward, backward, to the side, diagonally forward, or diagonally backward. If a dancer is facing north, a forward step will be to the north, a backward step to the south, a side step on the right foot to the east, a side step on the left foot to the west, diagonally forward on the right foot to the northeast, diagonally forward on the left foot to the northwest, diagonally backward on the right foot to the southeast, and diagonally backward on the left foot to the southwest.

TURNS

All turns will be described in terms of the direction and extent of the turn. For either partner, a right turn is clockwise and a left turn is counterclockwise. A *full* turn is a 360-degree turn; i.e., the dancer begins and ends the turn facing in the same direction. A *half* turn is a 180-degree turn in which the dancer finishes facing in the opposite direction from where he began. Similarly, a *quarter* turn is a 90-degree turn through a right angle, and an *eighth* turn is a 45-degree turn. In other words, if a dancer is originally facing north, after a full turn he again faces north; after a half turn, he faces south; after a quarter turn right, he faces east, and after an eighth turn right, he faces northeast.

When turns are described in this book for the various dances, we must emphasize that the fractions given are approximate. Often the degree of turn will be modified during a dance, depending on the position of other couples on the dance floor, on the amount of progression desired, and on Line of Dance.

ARCH TURN: An Arch Turn is a full turn left for the man and a full turn right for the woman, either individually or together. It is made through an arch formed by the woman's right arm and the man's left arm. To lead a woman into an Arch Turn, the man raises her right hand directly over her head and leads her into the turn right with gentle pressure from his right hand on her back. It is not necessary to *push* your partner! *Hold her right hand loosely, so that her fingers move inside your hand as she makes her turn*; if you grasp her hand too firmly, you will literally twist her wrist. A man's Arch Turn is similar; he holds the woman's right hand directly over his own head, again being sure that her fingers are free to turn inside his hand. In most cases, an Arch Turn is done in place — that is, without "travel." This is usually controlled by alternately turning the "inside" foot in place and stepping around it in a circle with the "outside" foot.

Arch Turn (a)

Arch Turn (b)

LOOP TURN: A Loop Turn is a full turn left for the woman or a full turn right for the man. To lead a woman into a Loop Turn, the man raises her right arm directly over her head. A man's Loop Turn is made by raising his left hand in front of his face with palm directly up. The woman's right hand is held over his head with fingers turning loosely until his turn is completed. The Loop Turn is also done in place with one foot serving as an axis.

Loop Turn

SOLO TURNS: A Solo Turn is a full turn made without contact between the partners. To lead a solo turn, the man lowers the clasped hands to waist level with palms down and then releases the woman's hand with a flick. Solo Turns may be done individually or together. Again, one foot is turned in place to avoid "travel" and arms are kept at shoulder level with palms down.

Left-hand Lead to Solo Turns

LINE OF DANCE (LOD)

Line of Dance or Line of Direction is an imaginary line running counter-clockwise around the outside of the dance floor. For *progressive* or *moving* dances, such as the waltz, fox-trot, polka, tango, and merengue, it is customary always to follow Line of Dance. It is a matter of courtesy to other dancers on the floor, and if everyone follows this progression there is less likelihood of interference or collision between couples.

In *spot* dances, such as the Lindy and cha-cha, it is customary to "stake out" a small area of the dance floor where partners remain throughout the number.

A real problem arises when different dances are done at the same time. For example, some couples will dance a Lindy to fox-trot music so that there is a combination of progressive and spot dancers competing for the same floor space. A similar situation arises when a fox-trot is danced to today's very slow "music to hug by" at the same time that other couples are standing in one place and simply swaying back and forth.

Music

For a dance to exist, there must first be music. This obvious statement implies that an understanding of music is essential to a dancer. Yet, strangely enough, most ballroom dancers and many teachers have very little knowledge of music. They keep time automatically but would be hard pressed to explain how their movements are actually tied into the music of a particular dance.

Music uses a system of symbols and notation to express its basic components, such as pitch, meter, and rhythm. *Pitch* defines the sound of a musical note; it is important for the enjoyment of music but does not itself affect the *rhythm* (timing) of a dance. The chief concern of the dancer is to know the *value* of musical notes and how they are grouped together to determine the rhythm.

In musical notation, the basic symbol is a *whole note*, which normally has a value of four beats of music. Similarly, a *half note* represents two beats, a *quarter note* one beat, and an *eighth note* half a beat. A dot after a note increases its value by one half. As an example here's a typical bar of musical notation:

The numbers 4/4 represent the metric signature or time signature: The top number gives the number of beats in a measure and the bottom number gives the value of each beat. In 4/4 time, there are four beats to a measure with a quarter note representing one beat. A vertical line, or *bar*, is used to separate the measures. Small wedges or *accent marks* are sometimes used to designate the accented beats. For example, in the fox-trot, the primary accent is on the first beat of the measure with a secondary accent on the third beat.

The first beat of the measure corresponds to the downward movement of a conductor's arm or baton; hence the term *downbeat* is often used for the first beat of a measure without reference to a conductor. Similarly, *upbeat* corresponds to the upward movement of a conductor's arm or baton and is often used to mean the last beat of a measure. The accented beats are called *strong* beats and the unaccented beats are called *weak* beats.

A feature of much dance music is syncopation, the deliberate distur-
bance of the normal pulse of meter, accent, and rhythm. The most common methods of achieving syncopation are: (a) tying an accented note to
the following weak note; (b) having rests on strong beats; (c) placing a stress
on the weak beat. In some dances such as the merengue and mambo,
syncopation determines the basic character of the dance. In other dances,
such as the Lindy, syncopation is commonly used to shift the accent to the
offbeat.

Ballroom dancing involves the fitting of appropriate dance figures to
the rhythm and melody of the music. This is known as *phrasing*. Dance
patterns are often described in terms of *quick* and *slow* steps; a *quick* step
occupies one beat of music and a *slow* step occupies two beats. However,
problems arise in such dances as the cha-cha, where there are eighth notes
occupying half a beat (these notes are sometimes referred to as *double-
quick*). Even worse is the samba, where there are sixteenth notes occupying
a quarter of a beat and dotted eighth notes occupying three quarters of a
beat. In this book, we shall use the standard system of *slow* and *quick* steps
wherever possible, but will give the actual value of each step where the
standard system breaks down.

Many dances, such as the polka, merengue, samba, and rumba, were
originally written in 2/4 time. Today these dances are almost always written
in "cut" time, or more properly *alla breve*, designated by the symbol ¢. This
time signature means that the half note is the basic unit of time rather than
the more commonly used quarter note. "Cut" time is usually equivalent to
2/2 time. A sample of the music might look as follows:

In "cut" time the first two quarter notes are played as the first beat and
the last two as the second beat of the measure. The advantage of "cut" time
is that it avoids subdivisions into eighth and sixteenth notes that are
required in 2/4 time. In general, music in "cut" time is easier to write and
much easier for the musicians to play. Practically all fast dance music,
including polka, Lindy, and Latin music, is written in "cut" time today.

Without intending to confuse the reader, we should point out that the
use of "cut" time does cause more problems in the definition of a *slow* or
quick step in dancing. For example, in the 4/4 time of fox-trot, two *slow* steps
are taken to one measure of music; thus each *slow* step corresponds to two
beats of music. Two *slow* steps are also taken to one measure in the Lindy,
but — since the Lindy is written in "cut" time — here one *slow* step
corresponds to one beat of music.

In the dance descriptions that follow, we avoid this question by breaking
down the individual figures into musical *counts*, using as a basis the number

of counts per measure commonly accepted for the dance in question. In some cases, such as the fox-trot and samba, the number of musical counts is the same as the number of beats per measure. In other dances, such as the Lindy and rumba, one beat is equal to two musical counts.

The entire subject of dance music is a complicated one. We have tried to simplify things as much as possible, but even trained musicians often have little real understanding of the basic musical features of the various dances they play so well.

An important consideration for ballroom dancers is the speed or *tempo* of a dance, usually expressed as the number of *measures per minute* of music (mpm). The United States Ballroom Council has established standard tempos for dance competition and also a tempo range for "enjoyable" social dancing, which we have used as a rough guide. For example, the "enjoyable" range for the American waltz is from 34–40 measures per minute, whereas the Viennese waltz ranges from 50–60 measures per minute.

In working with beginners, some teachers feel that slow music is easier since it gives more time to do the required movements. This is not always true, since with very slow music, the dancer is literally standing too long on one foot. Also, very slow music can change the entire character of a dance. It is a good idea, therefore, never to stray too far below the "enjoyable" range.

Terminology

In ballroom dancing today, knowledge of the language is just as important as mastery of the basic skills described above. You will find that there is a tendency on the part of the larger dance studios to assign their own terms to certain maneuvers and figures; terminology may also vary from one part of the country to the other. The following definitions are based in general on the efforts of Dance Educators of America and Dance Masters of America to achieve standardization and thus avoid confusion on the part of both the beginner and the more advanced ballroom dancer.

ARCH TURN: A turn to the right for the woman and to the left for the man, individually or together, through an arch formed by joined hands (woman's right and man's left hand).

BALL CHANGE: A transfer of weight from ball of one foot to flat of other foot.

BRUSH: To lightly touch inside edge of supporting foot with inside edge of free foot between changes of weight.

CHALLENGE POSITION: Partners face each other about a step apart with no contact.

CHASSÉ: Three changes of weight with a close on the second; also a series of sideward closes.

CLOSE: To move free foot next to supporting foot with one change of weight.

CLOSED POSITION: Partners face each other in conventional dance position; i.e., shoulders parallel, woman slightly to man's right, elbows away from body, man's right hand below woman's left shoulder blade; man holds woman's right hand in his left, and woman's left palm rests on his right shoulder.

COMMANDO: A forward or backward rock and close.

CONTRARY BODY MOVEMENT: A movement of the body, the action of turning the opposite hip and shoulder toward the direction of the moving leg; it is used to begin all turning movements.

CONTRARY BODY MOVEMENT POSITION: A *foot* position attained when either foot is placed across the front or back of the body without the body turning; every step taken outside partner must be placed in such a way that the two bodies remain parallel.

CORTÉ: In tango, a stop and change of direction forward or backward.

COUNTER PROMENADE POSITION: Man's left hip and woman's right hip are in or near contact, and the opposite sides of their bodies are opened out to form a compact "V"; man's right arm may be slightly extended to allow more freedom of movement (the opposite of Promenade Position).

CUBAN MOTION: A discreet but expressive hip movement achieved by bending and straightening the knees with carefully timed weight transfer.

CUDDLE POSITON: (also known as *Varsouvienne* or Skating Position): Woman is at man's left or right side, both facing in same direction; one arm of man is across woman's back, and position of other arm depends on method of arriving in Cuddle Position.

CUT: A basic foot movement in samba.

"CUT" TIME: A time signature in which the half note is the basic unit rather than the quarter note. It is usually equivalent to 2/2 time and is found in practically all fast dance music today.

DOWNBEAT: The first beat in a measure, corresponding to the downward movement of a conductor's arm or baton.

DRAW: To slowly move free foot to supporting foot without change of weight.

FAN: In tango, a half turn done on the ball of one foot while the free foot is kept directly behind the foot on which the turn is made.

FIGURE: A movement in social dancing in which a prescribed set of steps or pattern is completed.

FREE FOOT: The foot on which there is no weight.

LEFT OUTSIDE POSITION: Similar to Closed Position with shoulders parallel, woman positioned to man's left side backing in direction he is facing; a step forward on the left foot is placed outside the partner's left side.

LINE OF DIRECTION: (also known as Line of Dance): The counterclockwise course followed by dancers progressing around a room.

LOOP TURN: An individual turn to the left for the woman or to the right for the man.

OPEN BREAK POSITION: Partners face each other one or two steps apart with man holding woman's right hand in his left.

OPEN COUNTER PROMENADE POSITION: Partners are about one step apart, opened out so their bodies from a wide "V" opening to the man's right, with man holding woman's right hand in his left (opposite of Open Promenade Position).

OPEN PROMENADE POSITION: Partners are about one step apart, opened out so their bodies form a wide "V" opening to the man's left, with man holding woman's left hand in his right.

PHRASING: The fitting of dance figures to the rhythm and/or melody of the music. Phrasing may be adjusted in certain dances by the use of lead-in steps to bring the dancers in on a different beat.

PIVOT: A turning movement during which the free foot is kept either in front or directly behind the foot on which the turn is made. A pivot is a non-progressive turning step — it takes a series of pivots to progress.

PROGRESSIVE DANCE: A dance in which couples move along Line of Direction around the dance floor, as opposed to a *spot* dance.

PROMENADE POSITION: Man's right hip and woman's left hip are in or near contact, and the opposite sides of their bodies open out to form a compact "V."

RHYTHM: The regular occurrence of accented beats that shape the character of music or dance.

RIGHT OUTSIDE POSITION: Similar to Closed Position with shoulders parallel, woman positioned to man's right side backing in direction he is facing; a step forward on the right foot is placed outside the partner's right side.

RISE-AND-FALL: A controlled raising and lowering of the body while dancing.

ROCK: Two changes of weight, each in opposite directions.

SPIN: A turn done in place on the ball of one foot.

SPOT DANCE: A dance in which there is little or no movement along a Line of Direction, as opposed to a *progressive* dance.

SPOT TURN: A turn done in place using both feet — usually done as a couple.

STACCATO: A musical direction to perform a note quickly, lightly, and separated from the notes before or after it.

STEP: One change of weight.

SUPPORTING FOOT: The foot on which there is weight.

SWAY: To incline the whole body to one side from the feet upward, as opposed to bending from the waist.

SWIVEL: A twisting motion on the ball of one or both feet, *or* a turn on the ball of the supporting foot while the free foot is brought to a new position.

SYNCOPATION: A variation of the regular occurrence of accented beats within the framework of a basic rhythmic pattern.

TEMPO: Speed of the music, expressed for ballroom dancing in measures per minute.

TRIPLE: Three steps to two beats of music.

TURN: A turning movement in which the feet alternate.

TWINKLE: A step in any direction followed by a close and a step in another direction.

UPBEAT: The last beat of a measure, as opposed to *downbeat*.

III

THE
DANCES TODAY

The American Waltz

$\frac{3}{4}$ ♩ ♩ ♩ | ♩ ♩ ♩ |

For almost two centuries, the waltz has been the best known and most loved of all ballroom dances. Waltz music is written in three-quarter time with the first beat of each measure accented. Three types of waltz have been defined, depending on the tempo of the music: (1) The American waltz, once known as the Boston, is played at about 30–40 measures per minute and is the waltz most often danced in the United States today. (2) The Viennese waltz, played at between 50 and 60 measures per minute, is the waltz of Johann Strauss and other nineteenth-century composers. It is a very fast dance with couples turning continuously along the Line of Dance. (3) The International waltz, developed in England in the twentieth century, is played at a set tempo of 31 measures per minute (its figures are far more complicated and require considerable skill and practice).

The waltz is a progressive dance that requires smooth and continuous movement along Line of Dance. It is characterized by erect posture and *rise-and-fall*; that is, the first step of each measure is taken with bent knee and followed on the second and third steps by both partners rising to full height on the balls of their feet. Forward steps are taken on the heel and directly toward the partner. On side steps, both partners *sway* slightly away from their direction of travel (step left, sway right; step right, sway left). Partners stay fairly close together and take long reaching steps.

The following are several of the most popular waltz figures, beginning with those you will learn most easily. Remember that directions for turns are approximate and may be adjusted with regard to Line of Dance and the position of other couples on the dance floor. For example, the Forward Twinkles (Figure No. 5) are progressive if quarter turns are made; if half turns are made, the couple will simply move back and forth in the same place with no progression.

American Waltz Figure No. 1
Basic Waltz Box

3/4 time
Recommended measures per minute:
30–40
2 measures or 6 musical counts.

COUNT	MAN'S PART	WOMAN'S PART
1	From Closed Position (leaning forward slightly in anticipation of accented beat or *downbeat*), step forward on left foot and begin to rise to ball of foot at end of Count 1.	Reach back onto ball of right foot and lower to heel; begin to rise to ball of foot at end of Count 1.
2	Step to side on ball of right foot, now stretching to full height (body will sway to left).	Step to side on ball of left foot, now stretching to full height (body will sway to right).
3	Close left foot to right foot; transfer weight to left foot, continuing in *rise* position until end of Count 3.	Close right foot to left foot; transfer weight to right foot, continuing in *rise* position until end of Count 3.
4	On accented beat, reach back onto ball of right foot and lower to heel; begin to rise to ball of foot at end of Count 4.	Step forward on left foot; begin to rise to ball of foot at end of Count 4.
5	Step to side on ball of left foot as you stretch to full height (body will sway to right).	Step to side on ball of right foot as you stretch to full height (body will sway to left).
6	Close right foot to left foot; transfer weight to right foot, continuing in *rise* position until end of Count 6.	Close left foot to right foot; transfer weight to left foot, continuing in *rise* position until end of Count 6.

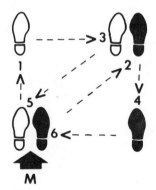

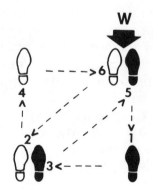

Count 1

Count 2

Count 3

Count 4

Count 5

Count 6

The waltz is a turning dance, and a quarter turn to the left by the man on the accented beats (Counts 1 and 4) comes quite naturally. A firm hold on his partner will be all she needs to follow this *turning basic* figure. Just as easily, this Basic Waltz Box becomes a *forward basic* if the man steps forward on Count 4 (the woman stepping back).

American Waltz Figure No. 2
The Hesitation

3/4 time
Recommended measures per minute:
30–40
2 measures or 6 musical counts

COUNT	MAN'S PART	WOMAN'S PART
1	From Closed Position, step to side on left foot; transfer weight to left foot and begin to rise to ball of foot at end of Count 1.	Step to side on right foot; transfer weight to right foot and begin to rise to ball of foot at end of Count 1.
2	Stretch to full height (weight remains on left foot).	Stretch to full height (weight remains on right foot).
3	*Draw* right foot to left foot without a transfer of weight and continue in *rise* position until end of Count 3.	*Draw* left foot to right foot without a transfer of weight and continue in *rise* position until end of Count 3.
4	Step to side on right foot; transfer weight to right foot and begin to rise to ball of foot at end of Count 4.	Step to side on left foot; transfer weight to left foot and begin to rise to ball of foot at end of Count 4.
5	Stretch to full height (weight remains on right foot).	Stretch to full height (weight remains on left foot).
6	*Draw* left foot to right foot without a transfer of weight and continue in *rise* position until end of Count 6.	*Draw* right foot to left foot without a transfer of weight and continue in *rise* position until end of Count 6.

Count 1 Count 2 Count 3

Count 4 Count 5 Count 6

The Hesitation may be done to either side or backward or forward as often as needed to recover balance or change pace. It is particularly useful in a very fast waltz, such as the Viennese style.

American Waltz Figure No. 3
Simple Twinkle

3/4 time
Recommended measures per minute:
30–40
2 measures or 6 musical counts

COUNT	MAN'S PART	WOMAN'S PART
1	From Closed Position, step forward on left foot and begin to rise to ball of foot at end of Count 1.	Reach back onto ball of right foot and lower to heel; begin to rise to ball of foot at end of Count 1.
2	Step to side on ball of right foot, now stretching to full height.	Step to side on ball of left foot, now stretching to full height.
3	Close left foot to right foot, making ⅛ turn left and using heel of right hand to lead partner into Promenade Position (in *rise* position until end of Count 3).	Close right foot to left foot, making ⅛ turn right into Promenade Position (in *rise* position until end of Count 3).
4	Cross right foot in front of left foot; both partners are now on "inside" foot and begin to rise at end of Count 4.	Cross left foot in front of right foot; both partners are now on "inside" foot and begin to rise at end of Count 4.
5	Step to side on ball of left foot, making ⅛ turn right and leading partner back to Closed Position as you both rise to full height.	Step to side on ball of right foot, making ⅛ turn left to face partner in Closed Position as you both rise to full height.
6	Close right foot to left foot; transfer weight to right foot and continue in *rise* position until end of Count 6.	Close left foot to right foot; transfer weight to left foot and continue in *rise* position until end of Count 6.

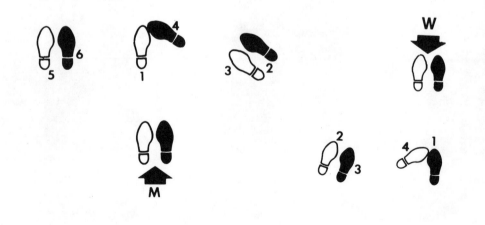

Count 1

Count 2

Count 3

Count 4

Count 5

Count 6

American Waltz Figure No. 4
Arch Turn for Woman

3/4 time
Recommended measures per minute:
  30–40
4 measures or 12 musical counts

COUNT	MAN'S PART	WOMAN'S PART
1–3	Complete first three counts of Basic Waltz Box (Figure No. 1).	Same.
4	Step back on right foot, *toeing in*.	Step forward on left foot.
5	Step to side on left foot, beginning ¼ turn left (to be completed in two steps) and raising left hand to turn partner's right hand over her head in an *arch* as your right hand on her back leads her into first step of ½ turn to her right.	Step forward on right foot, making ¼ turn to right.
6	Close right foot to left foot, completing ¼ turn left as you lead partner around in final step of her turn right.	Step back on left foot, making ¼ turn right.
7	Step to side on left foot, making ¼ turn left to face partner in Closed Position.	Step back on right foot.
8	Step to side on right foot.	Step to side on left foot.
9	Close left foot to right foot.	Close right foot to left foot.
10–12	Complete final three counts of Basic Waltz Box (Figure No. 1).	Complete final three counts of Basic Waltz Box (Figure No. 1).

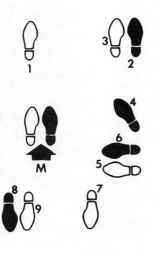

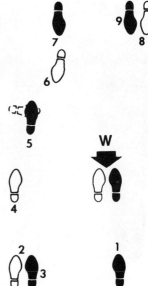

Count 1

Count 2

Count 3

Count 4

Count 5

Count 6

Count 7

American Waltz Figure No. 5
Forward Twinkles

3/4 time
Recommended measures per minute:
30–40
4 measures or 12 musical counts

COUNT	MAN'S PART	WOMAN'S PART
1	From Closed Position, step forward on left foot.	Step back on right foot.
2	Step to side on right foot, *beginning* ⅛ turn left.	Step to side on left foot, *beginning* ⅛ turn left.
3	Close left foot to right foot as you complete ⅛ turn left into Right Outside Position.	Close right foot to left foot as you complete ⅛ turn left into Right Outside Position.
4	Step forward on right foot.	Step back on left foot.
5	Step to side on left foot, beginning ¼ turn right.	Step to side on right foot, beginning ¼ turn right.
6	Close right foot to left foot as you complete ¼ turn right into Left Outside Position.	Close left foot to right foot as you complete ¼ turn right into Left Outside Position.
7	Step forward on left foot.	Step back on right foot.
8	Step to side on right foot, beginning ¼ turn left.	Step to side on left foot, beginning ¼ turn left.
9	Close left foot to right foot as you complete ¼ turn left into Right Outside Position.	Close right foot to left foot as you complete ¼ turn right into Right Outside Position.
10	Step forward on right foot.	Step back on left foot.
11	Step to side on left foot, beginning ¼ turn right to repeat Counts 5 through 10 *or* making ⅛ turn right to resume Closed Position.	Step to side on right foot, beginning ¼ turn right to repeat Counts 5 through 10 *or* making ⅛ turn right to Closed Position.
12	Close right foot to left foot.	Close left foot to right foot.

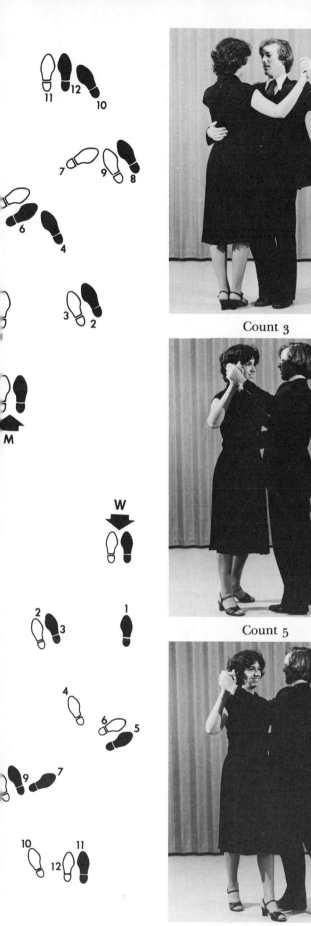

Count 3

Count 4

Count 5

Count 6

Count 7

Count 8

American Waltz Figure No. 6
The Beanbag

3/4 time
Recommended measures per minute:
30–40
4 measures or 12 musical counts

COUNT	MAN'S PART	WOMAN'S PART
1–4	Complete first four counts of Simple Twinkle (Figure No. 3).	Same.
5	With left foot, take long step across partner (releasing her right hand as you face her), making ½ turn right and placing left hand on her back.	Step forward on right foot with toe pointing between partner's feet as he steps across.
6	Making quick turn right into Counter Promenade Position, step forward on right foot.	Step forward on left foot in Counter Promenade Position.
7	Step through on left (inside) foot.	Step through on right (inside) foot.
8	Step forward on right foot with toe pointing between partner's feet as you lead her across to your right; drop left hand and place right hand on her back.	With left foot, take long step across partner, making ½ turn right.
9	Bringing partner into Promenade Position with right-hand lead, step forward on left foot.	Making quick turn right into Promenade Position, step forward on right foot.
10	Step forward on right (inside) foot.	Step forward on left (inside) foot.
11	Step to side on left foot, bringing partner to Closed Position with strong right-hand lead.	Step to side on right foot, making ½ turn left to face partner in Closed Position.
12	Close right foot to left foot.	Close left foot to right foot.

Count 4

Count 5

Count 6

Count 7

Count 8

Count 9

Count 10

Count 11

Count 12

Copyrighted in 1914, this piece is probably the first ever published specifically for the fox-trot.

The Fox-Trot

$$\frac{4}{4} \quad \downarrow \quad \downarrow \quad \downarrow \quad \downarrow \mid \downarrow \quad \downarrow \quad \downarrow \quad \downarrow \mid$$

The fox-trot is written in 4/4 time, with the primary accent on the first beat of the measure and a secondary accent on the third beat. Each measure has four separate and distinct beats. The variability of rhythm found in the fox-trot makes it a continuously interesting dance. The two most popular rhythms are *slow-slow-quick-quick*, which requires one and a half measures or six musical counts, and *slow-quick-quick*, which requires one measure or four musical counts. There are several types of fox-trot: (1) Slow to medium fox-trots for enjoyable dancing — and best for beginners — are played at 25–45 measures per minute. (2) A fast fox-trot or *Peabody*, played at 55–66 measures per minute, includes frequent cross-steps and outside position. (3) The *International* (English) *quickstep* is played at 50 measures per minute, and while the figures themselves are not exceptionally difficult, they are challenging because of the tempo of the dance. (4) The graceful *Roseland* fox-trot is played at medium tempo and combines a *quick-quick-slow* rhythm with frequent use of outside position. (5) The very slow fox-trot, sometimes called "music to hug by."

The fox-trot is a progressive dance that requires smooth and controlled movement along Line of Dance. Long gliding and perfectly smooth steps give the dance its casual and unhurried look. Carriage is erect, knees are soft, and there is no motion above the hips. The heel leads on slow forward steps, and all quick steps are taken on the ball of the foot. Characteristic of the fox-trot is the *brush*, a follow-through motion originally used in the two-step. When making a step to the side, the free foot brushes the supporting foot and then steps directly to the side.

You will find that many waltz figures, particularly the Simple Twinkle, Forward Twinkles, and Beanbag covered in the preceding chapter, are quite easily adapted to *slow-quick-quick* fox-trot (Figure No. 7).

In social dancing, the man is free to combine any fox-trot figures he may choose, moving from one rhythm to another in a way that keeps fox-trot one of our most enjoyable and stimulating dances year after year. You must remember, however, that learning to lead and follow smoothly from one rhythm to another requires practice and can be a real challenge for the woman, who must be ready to adjust instantly to the changes.

Fox-Trot Figure No. 1
Slow-Slow-Quick-Quick Basic

4/4 Time
Recommended measures per minute:
25–45
1½ measures or 6 musical counts

COUNT	MAN'S PART	WOMAN'S PART
1–2	SLOW: From Closed Position, lean forward slightly and then (on the *downbeat*) take a normal walking step on left foot.	SLOW: Reaching back from your waist, step back on ball of right foot.
3–4	SLOW: Step forward on right foot.	SLOW: Step back on left foot.
5	QUICK: Step directly to side on left foot, "brushing" right ankle on the way. Hold partner firmly.	QUICK: Step directly to side on right foot, "brushing" left ankle on the way.
6	QUICK: Close right foot to left foot, transferring weight to right foot in preparation for the next figure.	QUICK: Close left foot to right foot, transferring weight to left foot in preparation for the next figure.

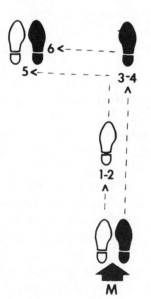
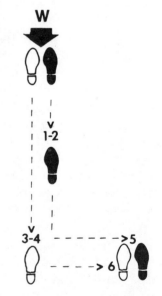

Counts 1–2

Counts 3–4

Count 5

Count 6

Fox-Trot Figure No. 2
Forward Basic

4/4 time
Recommended measures per minute:
25–45
1½ measures or 6 musical counts

COUNT	MAN'S PART	WOMAN'S PART
1–2	SLOW: From Closed Position, step forward on left foot.	SLOW: Step back on right foot.
3–4	SLOW: Step forward on right foot.	SLOW: Step back on left foot.
5	QUICK: Step forward on ball of left foot.	QUICK: Step back on right foot.
6	QUICK: Step forward on ball of right foot.	QUICK: Step back on left foot.

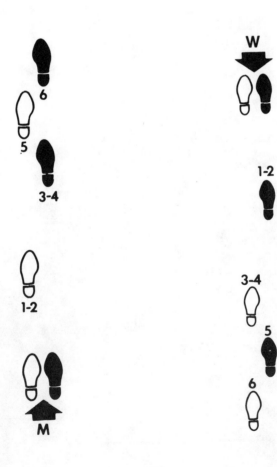

Counts 1–2

Counts 3–4

Count 5

Count 6

Fox-Trot Figure No. 3
The Conversation

4/4 time
Recommended measures per minute:
25–45
1½ measures or 6 musical counts

COUNT	MAN'S PART	WOMAN'S PART
1–2	SLOW: From Closed Position, step to side on left foot, making ⅛ turn left and using gentle pressure with heel of your right hand to lead partner into Promenade Position.	SLOW: Step to side on right foot, making ⅛ turn right into Promenade Position.
3–4	SLOW: Cross right foot in front of left foot.	SLOW: Cross left foot in front of right foot.
5	QUICK: Step to side on left foot, making ⅛ turn right to face partner in Closed Position.	QUICK: Step to side on right foot, making ⅛ turn left to face partner in Closed Position.
6	QUICK: Close right foot to left foot.	QUICK: Close left foot to right foot.

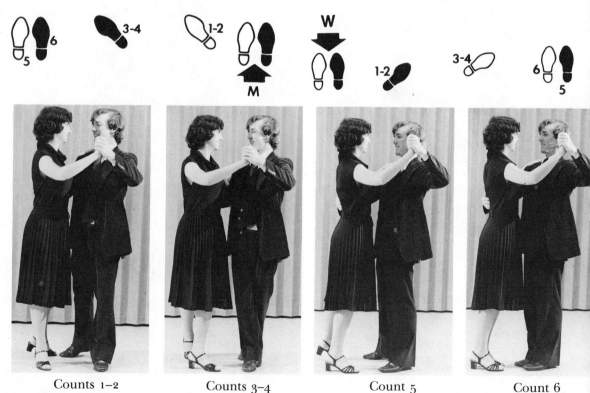

Counts 1–2   Counts 3–4   Count 5   Count 6

Fox-Trot Figure No. 4

The Conversation with Arch Turn for Woman

4/4 time
Recommended measures per minute:
  25–45
3 measures or 12 musical counts

COUNT	MAN'S PART	WOMAN'S PART
1–6	Complete all counts of The Conversation (Figure No. 3).	Same
7–8	SLOW: Step to side on left foot, turning left into Promenade Position; raise left hand and turn partner's right hand over her head in an *arch* as your right hand on her back leads her into ½ turn to her right (the first step of a full turn).	SLOW: Step to side on right foot, making ½ turn right (the first step of a full turn).
9–10	SLOW: Cross right foot in front of left foot as you continue turning partner to her right.	SLOW: Step to side on left foot, making ½ turn right.
11	QUICK: Step to side on left foot and resume Closed Position.	QUICK: Step to side on right foot to face partner in Closed Position.
12	QUICK: Close right foot to left foot.	QUICK: Close left foot to right foot.

| Counts 7–8 | Counts 9–10 | Count 11 | Count 12 |

Fox-Trot Figure No. 5
Left Rock Turns

4/4 time
Recommended measures per minute:
25–45
1½ measures or 6 musical counts

COUNT	MAN'S PART	WOMAN'S PART
1–2	SLOW: From Closed Position, *rock* forward on left foot, anticipating turn to left (with firm hold on partner).	SLOW: *Rock* back on right foot.
3–4	SLOW: Replace weight on right foot, beginning to make turn to left.	SLOW: Replace weight on left foot, beginning to make turn to left.
5	QUICK: Step to side on left foot, completing ¼ turn left.	QUICK: Step to side on right foot, completing ¼ turn left.
6	QUICK: Close right foot to left foot.	QUICK: Close left foot to right foot.

Counts 1–2

Counts 3–4

Count 5

Count 6

Fox-Trot Figure No. 6
The Park Avenue

4/4 time
Recommended measures per minute:
25–45
3 measures or 12 musical counts

COUNT	MAN'S PART	WOMAN'S PART
1–2	SLOW: From Closed Position, step diagonally forward on left foot into Right Outside Position.	SLOW: Step diagonally back on right foot into Right Outside Position.
3–4	SLOW: Step forward on right foot.	SLOW: Step back on left foot.
5	QUICK: Step to side on left foot, making turn right into Closed Position.	QUICK: Step to side on right foot, making turn right into Closed Position.
6	QUICK: Close right foot to left foot, making turn right into Left Outside Position.	QUICK: Close left foot to right foot, making turn right into Left Outside Position.
7–8	SLOW: Step back on left foot.	SLOW: Step forward on right foot.
9–10	SLOW: Step back on right foot.	SLOW: Step forward on left foot.
11	QUICK: Step to side on left foot, making turn left into Closed Position.	QUICK: Step to side on right foot, making turn left into Closed Position.
12	QUICK: Close right foot to left foot.	QUICK: Close left foot to right foot.

Counts 1–2

Counts 3–4

Count 5

Count 6

Counts 7–8

Counts 9–10

Count 11

Count 12

Fox-Trot Figure No. 7
Slow-Quick-Quick Basic

4/4 time
Recommended measures per minute:
25–45
2 measures or 8 musical counts

COUNT	MAN'S PART	WOMAN'S PART
1–2	SLOW: From Closed Position, step forward on left foot.	SLOW: Step back on right foot.
3	QUICK: Step to side on right foot (remembering to "brush" left ankle).	QUICK: Step to side on left foot (remembering to "brush" right ankle).
4	QUICK: Close left foot to right foot.	QUICK: Close right foot to left foot.
5–6	SLOW: Step back on right foot.	SLOW: Step forward on left foot.
7	QUICK: Step to side on left foot.	QUICK: Step to side on right foot.
8	QUICK: Close right foot to left foot.	QUICK: Close left foot to right foot.

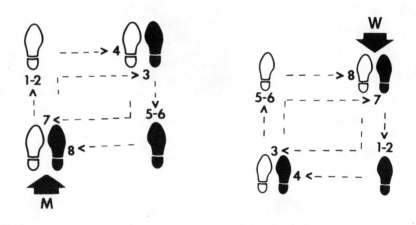

This figure becomes a *turning basic* by making a turn to the left on the slow steps. It becomes a *forward basic* by substituting a forward step for the man on Counts 5–6. Once you are accustomed to the slow-quick-quick rhythm of fox-trot, you will be able to use all of the waltz figures given in this book, such as Forward Twinkles and The Beanbag.

Counts 1–2

Count 3

Count 4

Counts 5–6

Count 7

Count 8

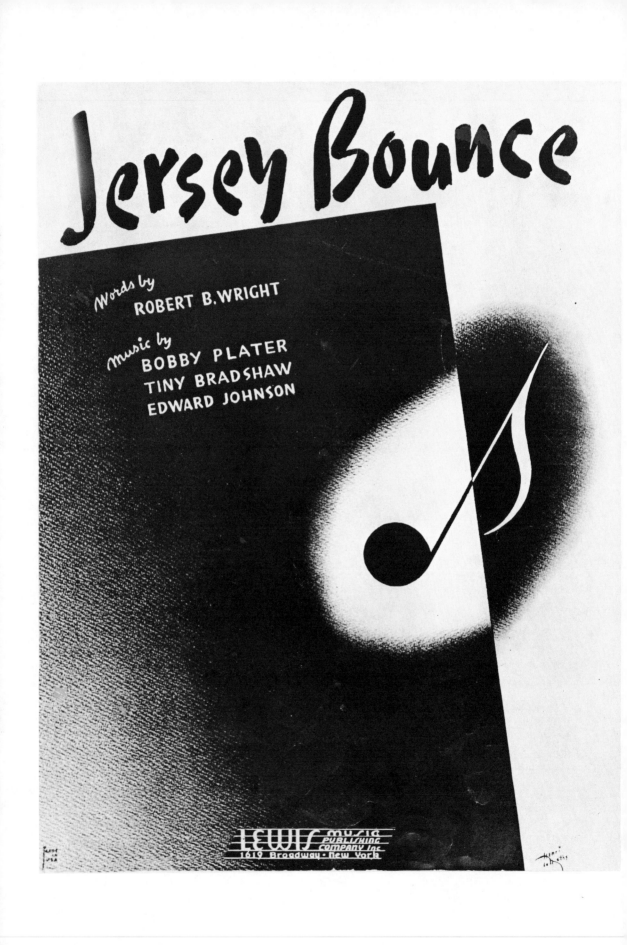

The Lindy

The Lindy (also known as *swing*, *jitterbug*, and *jive*) is written in "cut" time (2/2) as contrasted with the 4/4 time of fox-trot. This lively dance has more freedom of style than any other ballroom dance, and posture is unimportant. Its many versions include *Single Lindy*, *Double Lindy*, *Triple Lindy*, six-count, eight-count, eastern, western, and so forth. Lindy is a *spot* dance, where each couple stakes out a small territory on the dance floor and does "its own thing."

A unique characteristic of the Lindy is its hand-hold. The woman's right hand is held palm down with fingers slightly curled; the man's left hand is held with palm up, and his fingers curl slightly to fit hers and form the *tension hold* needed for the many turns and changes of position. His thumb is held loosely over the back of the woman's right hand. The dance is begun in Promenade (or Semi-open) Position, with the hands joined at about waist level.

The *Single Lindy* is danced to a six-count *slow-slow-quick-quick* rhythm. It can be done to music ranging from 34–48 measures per minute, depending on the agility of the dancers. In *Triple Lindy*, where three steps are taken to two counts of music, the *triple* is danced as follows: *double-quick* (one-half count), *double-quick* (one-half count), *quick* (one count). The *Triple Lindy* is usually done to slower music, ranging from 30–40 measures per minute.

As soon as you are comfortable with *Single Lindy* rhythm and can handle the changes of position in the first four figures that follow, you will be ready for the fun of *Triple Lindy* (Figure No. 5). For most Lindy figures, as in the first four in this chapter, the two rhythms are interchangeable, although you will soon develop favorite figures for each rhythm and tempo. For example, the *Sugarfoot Walk* (Figure No. 6) seems to us most effective in the rhythm of *Triple Lindy*.

Lindy Figure No. 1

Single Lindy Basic

2/2 ("cut") time
Recommended measures per minute:
34–48
1½ measures or 6 musical counts

COUNT	MAN'S PART	WOMAN'S PART
1–2	SLOW: From Promenade Position with left hand at waist level and thumb on back of partner's right hand, step to side on left foot.	SLOW: Step to side on right foot.
3–4	SLOW: Step in place on right foot.	SLOW: Step in place on left foot.
5	QUICK: Cross left foot in back of right foot, rocking back on ball of left foot.	QUICK: Cross right foot in back of left foot, rocking back on ball of right foot.
6	QUICK: Replace weight on right foot, resuming Promenade Position.	QUICK: Replace weight on left foot, resuming Promenade Position.

Counts 1–2

Counts 3–4

Count 5

Count 6

The above figure becomes a *turning basic* when the man makes a quarter turn to the right on Count 1–2. The woman does not turn, and the couple remains in Closed Position until Count 5.

Lindy Figure No. 2

Arch Turn for Woman to Open Break Position

2/2 ("cut") time
Recommended measures per minute:
34–48
3 measures or 12 musical counts

COUNT	MAN'S PART	WOMAN'S PART
1–6	Complete all six counts of Single Lindy Basic (Figure No. 1).	Same.
7–8	SLOW: Step to side on left foot, raising left hand and turning partner's right hand in an *arch* over her head as your right hand on her back leads her in first step of ¾ turn to her right.	SLOW: Step to side on right foot, making turn right (the first step of a ¾ turn).
9–10	SLOW: Step to side on right foot as you continue to turn partner to her right.	SLOW: Step forward on left foot, completing ¾ turn to right to face partner.
11	QUICK: Rock directly back on ball of left foot in Open Break Position.	QUICK: Rock directly back on ball of right foot in Open Break Position.
12	QUICK: Replace weight on right foot, remaining in Open Break Position with partner's right hand in your left hand.	QUICK: Replace weight on left foot to remain in Open Break Position.

Counts 7–8   Counts 9–10   Count 11   Count 12

Lindy Figure No. 3

Arch Turn to Loop Turn for Woman

2/2 ("cut") time
Recommended measures per minute:
  34–48
4½ measures or 18 musical counts

COUNT	MAN'S PART	WOMAN'S PART
1–12	Complete all twelve counts of Arch Turn for Woman to Open Break Position (Figure No. 2).	Same.
13–14	SLOW: Step to side on left foot, making ½ turn right as you raise left hand to *loop* partner in ½ turn to her left by drawing her right hand across her face and then over her head (your hand turning loosely inside of hers).	SLOW: Step to side on right foot, making ½ turn left.
15–16	SLOW: Close right foot to left foot, completing your turn to face partner after changing places with her.	SLOW: Step back on left foot, completing turn to face partner after changing places with him.
17	QUICK: Rock back on ball of left foot in Open Break Position.	QUICK: Rock back on ball of right foot in Open Break Position.
18	QUICK: Replace weight on right foot.	QUICK: Replace weight on left foot.

Count 12

Counts 13–14

Counts 15–16

Count 17

Count 18

Lindy Figure No. 4
She Go, He Go

2/2 ("cut") time
Recommended measures per minute:
  34–48
1½ measures or 6 musical counts

COUNT	MAN'S PART	WOMAN'S PART
1–2	SLOW: From Open Break Position (following either Figure No. 2 or No. 3), step to side on left foot, raising left hand to *loop* partner in ½ turn to her left by drawing her right hand across her face and then over her head (your hand turning loosely inside of hers).	SLOW: Step to side on right foot, making ½ turn left.
3–4	SLOW: Step to side on right foot, making ½ turn left under the *arch* and then lowering hands at end of count.	SLOW: Step back on left foot, completing turn to face partner after changing places with him.
5	QUICK: Rock back on ball of left foot in Open Break Position.	QUICK: Rock back on ball of right foot in Open Break Position.
6	QUICK: Replace weight on right foot.	QUICK: Replace weight on left foot.

Counts 1–2 (a)

Counts 1–2 (b)

Counts 3–4 (a)

Counts 3–4 (b)

Count 5

Count 6

2/2 ("cut") time
Recommended measures per minute:
30–40
1½ measures or 6 musical counts

COUNT	MAN'S PART	WOMAN'S PART
1–2	SLOW: From Promenade Position, take three short steps in a *Lindy chassé* (usually called a "triple") to the left, as follows: To side on left foot (½ count); closing right foot to left foot (½ count); to side on left foot (one full count).	SLOW: Take three short steps in a *Lindy chassé* (usually called a "triple") to the right, as follows: To side on right foot (½ count); closing left foot to right foot (½ count); to side on right foot (one full count).
3–4	SLOW: *Triple* to the right as follows: To side on right foot (½ count); closing left foot to right foot (½ count); to side on right foot (one full count).	SLOW: *Triple* to the left as follows: To side on left foot (½ count); closing right foot to left foot (½ count); to side on left foot (one full count).
5	QUICK: Cross left foot in back of right foot, rocking back.	QUICK: Cross right foot in back of left foot, rocking back.
6	QUICK: Replace weight on right foot, resuming Promenade Position.	QUICK: Replace weight on left foot, resuming Promenade Position.

Count 1 (a)

Count 1 (b)

Count 2

Count 3 (a)

Count 3 (b)

Count 4

Count 5

Count 6

Lindy Figure No. 6
Sugarfoot Walk

2/2 ("cut") time
Recommended measures per minute:
30–40
1½ measures or 6 musical counts

COUNT	MAN'S PART	WOMAN'S PART
1–2	SLOW: From Promenade Position, triple to left (left foot, right foot, left foot), removing right hand from partner's back and making ¼ turn left as you lower left hand and lead her across to your left.	SLOW: Triple forward (right foot, left foot, right foot), beginning to turn to left.
3–4	SLOW: Triple to right (right foot, left foot, right foot) as you lead partner in turn left to face you in Open Break Position.	SLOW: Triple forward (left foot, right foot, left foot), completing turn left to face partner in Open Break Position.
5	QUICK: Take small step back on left foot as you lead partner forward in her Sugarfoot Walk, curving slightly to the right.	QUICK: Step forward on right foot (with knee flexed and toeing out) and *swivel* to left (straightening knee and toeing in).
6	QUICK: Take small step back on right foot as you continue leading partner forward, curving slightly to right. Repeat Counts 5 and 6 two or three times, stepping forward on Count 6 when you wish to resume Promenade Position.	QUICK: Step forward on left foot (with knee flexed and toeing out) and *swivel* to right (straightening knee and toeing in).

Count 1   Count 2   Count 3 (a)

Count 3 (b)   Count 4

Count 5   Count 6

Lindy Figure No. 7
The Mooch

2/2 ("cut") time
Recommended measures per minute:
34–48
4 measures or 16 musical counts

COUNT	MAN'S PART	WOMAN'S PART
1–6	Complete all six counts of Single Lindy Basic (Figure No. 1).	Same.
7–8	SLOW: Kick left foot forward (pointing toe down); replace weight on left foot.	SLOW: Kick right foot forward (pointing toe down); replace weight on right foot.
9–10	SLOW: Kick right foot forward; replace weight on right foot, making turn right to Closed Position.	SLOW: Kick left foot forward; replace weight on left foot, making turn left to Closed Position.
11–12	SLOW: Kick left foot forward *outside* partner; replace weight on left foot.	SLOW: Kick right foot forward between partner's feet; replace weight on right foot.
13–14	SLOW: Kick right foot forward between partner's feet; replace weight on right foot.	SLOW: Kick left foot forward *outside* partner; replace weight on left foot.
15	QUICK: Cross left foot in back of right foot, rocking back.	QUICK: Cross right foot in back of left foot, rocking back.
16	QUICK: Replace weight on right foot, resuming Promenade Position.	QUICK: Replace weight on left foot, resuming Promenade Position.

Count 7

Count 9

Count 11

Count 13

Count 15

Count 16

SIX LESSONS FROM
MADAME LA ZONGA

Lyric by
CHARLES NEWMAN
Music by
JAMES V. MONACO

Featured by
JIMMY DORSEY
AND HIS ORCHESTRA
with **BOB EBERLY**
and **HELEN O'CONNELL**

BVC
BREGMAN, VOCCO and CONN, Inc.
1619 BROADWAY   NEW YORK, N.Y.

The American Rumba

¢ ♩ ♩ ♪ | ♩ ♩ ♪ |

Although the original Cuban rumba was in 2/4 time, the American rumba is almost always written in "cut" time. The melodic factor of rumba music comes from the drums, maracas, and claves. American rumba is a spot dance with a four-count *quick-quick-slow* rhythm. As with most Latin dances, it is done with flat feet, and dancers rise to the ball of the foot only for turning movements such as pivots. *All steps must be small*, and shoulders remain quiet throughout the dance. Free arms are held at about shoulder level with palms down ("armchair" position) and provide an important lead contact. The dance involves many solo turns, and it is essential to keep one foot in place as it turns so that you and your partner do not travel too far apart. The rumba is a dance where the man "shows off" his partner, and the woman maintains an erect and proud carriage as she moves smoothly from one figure to another.

Characteristic of all forms of rumba is Cuban Motion, which has been defined as "a discreet but expressive hip movement achieved by bending and straightening the knees with carefully timed weight transfer." The following exercise will help you: (a) With left knee slightly bent, take a small step to the side on the left foot, receiving the weight on the *inside* of the foot. (b) Gradually roll the left foot until weight is on the *outside*, at the same time straightening the left leg until you feel yourself "sit" on the left hip. (c) With right knee slightly bent, close right foot to left foot, receiving the weight on the *inside* of the right foot. (d) Gradually roll the right foot until weight is on the *outside*, at the same time straightening the right leg until you feel yourself "sit" on the right hip. Repeat the exercise in the opposite direction. Do not exaggerate. Remember that the hips should move only through knee action. Take the time to acquire a smooth and subtle Cuban Motion — it will serve you well in many Latin dances.

American Rumba Figure No. 1
Basic Rumba Box

2/2 ("cut") time
Recommended measures per minute:
28–34
2 measures or 8 musical counts

COUNT	MAN'S PART	WOMAN'S PART
1	QUICK: From Closed Position, with left knee slightly bent, take small step to side on left foot; transfer weight; *then* straighten left leg until you feel yourself "sit" on left hip. Hips move only through knee action, and shoulders remain quiet. *This is Cuban Motion.*	QUICK: With right knee slightly bent, take small step to side on right foot; transfer weight; *then* straighten right leg until you feel yourself "sit" on right hip. Hips move only through knee action, and shoulders remain quiet.
2	QUICK: With right knee slightly bent, close right foot to left foot; transfer weight and straighten leg until you "sit" on right hip.	QUICK: With left knee slightly bent, close left foot to right foot; transfer weight and straighten leg until you "sit" on left hip.
3–4	SLOW: With left knee slightly bent, take small step forward on left foot; transfer weight and straighten leg until you "sit" on left hip.	SLOW: With right knee slightly bent, take small step back on flat of right foot; transfer weight and straighten leg until you "sit" on right hip.
5	QUICK: Continuing with Cuban Motion, take small step to side on right foot.	QUICK: Continuing with Cuban Motion, take small step to side on left foot.
6	QUICK: Close left foot to right foot.	QUICK: Close right foot to left foot.
7–8	SLOW: Take small step back on flat of right foot.	SLOW: Take small step forward on left foot.

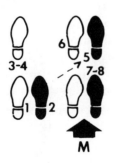
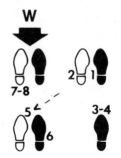

Count 1

Count 2

Counts 3–4

Count 5

Count 6

Counts 7–8

American Rumba Figure No. 2
Arch Turn for Woman

2/2 ("cut") time
Recommended measures per minute:
28–34
2 measures or 8 musical counts

COUNT	MAN'S PART	WOMAN'S PART
1	QUICK: From Closed Position, step to side on left foot, turning left into Promenade Position; raise left hand and turn partner's right hand in an *arch* as your right hand on her back leads her into turn to her right.	QUICK: Step to side on right foot, turning right into Promenade Position. (This is the first of six steps in a small circle to the right.)
2	QUICK: Close right foot to left foot (maintaining Cuban Motion) as you continue to lead partner to her right.	QUICK: Step forward on left foot, continuing to turn right (free arm always raised in "armchair" position).
3–4	SLOW: Step forward on left foot as you continue to lead partner to her right.	SLOW: Step forward on right foot, continuing to turn right.
5	QUICK: Step to side on right foot as you continue turning partner.	QUICK: Step forward on left foot, continuing to turn right.
6	QUICK: Close left foot to right foot as you continue turning partner.	QUICK: Step forward on right foot, continuing to turn right.
7–8	SLOW: Step back on right foot, turning right to bring partner to Closed Position.	SLOW: Step forward on left foot, making final turn to face partner in Closed Position.

Count 1

Count 2

Counts 3–4

Count 5

Count 6

Counts 7–8

American Rumba Figure No. 3
Forward Breaks

2/2 ("cut") time
Recommended measures per minute:
   28–34
4 measures or 16 musical counts

COUNT	MAN'S PART	WOMAN'S PART
1	QUICK: From Closed Position, step to side on left foot.	QUICK: Step to side on right foot.
2	QUICK: Close right foot to left foot.	QUICK: Close left foot to right foot.
3–4	SLOW: Step forward on left foot, making turn left into Right Outside Position.	SLOW: Step back on right foot, making turn left into Right Outside Position.
5	QUICK: Rock forward on right foot.	QUICK: Rock back on left foot.
6	QUICK: Replace weight on left foot.	QUICK: Replace weight on right foot.
7–8	SLOW: Step to side on right foot, making turn right into Closed Position.	SLOW: Step to side on left foot, making turn right into Closed Position.
9	QUICK: Rock forward on left foot into Left Outside Position.	QUICK: Rock back on right foot into Left Outside Position.
10	QUICK: Replace weight on right foot.	QUICK: Replace weight on left foot.
11–12	SLOW: Step to side on left foot, making turn left into Closed Position.	SLOW: Step to side on right foot, making turn left into Closed Position.
13	QUICK: Rock forward on right foot into Right Outside Position.	QUICK: Rock back on left foot into Right Outside Position.
14	QUICK: Replace weight on left foot.	QUICK: Replace weight on right foot.
15–16	SLOW: Step diagonally back on right foot, returning partner to Closed Position.	SLOW: Step directly forward on left foot to face partner in Closed Position.

Count 1

Count 2

Counts 3–4

Counts 5 and 13

Counts 6 and 14

Counts 7–8

Count 9

Count 10

Counts 11–12

2/2 ("cut") time
Recommended measures per minute:
28–34
6 measures or 24 musical counts

COUNT	MAN'S PART	WOMAN'S PART
1–4	QUICK-QUICK-SLOW: First four counts of Basic Rumba Box (Figure No. 1).	Same.
5	QUICK: Step to side on right foot.	QUICK: Step to side on left foot.
6	QUICK: Close left foot to right foot.	QUICK: Close right foot to left foot.
7–8	SLOW: Step to side on right foot.	SLOW: Step to side on left foot.
9	QUICK: Cross left foot in back of right foot, making ⅛ turn left and leading partner to Promenade Position.	QUICK: Cross right foot in back of left foot, making ⅛ turn right into Promenade Position.
10	QUICK: Step in place on right foot.	QUICK: Step in place on left foot.
11–12	SLOW: Step to side on left foot, making ⅛ turn right to Closed Position.	SLOW: Step to side on right foot, making ⅛ turn left to Closed Position.
13	QUICK: Cross right foot in back of left foot, making ¼ turn right and leading partner to Open Counter Promenade Position.	QUICK: Cross left foot in back of right foot, making ¼ turn left into Open Counter Promenade Position.
14	QUICK: Step in place on left foot.	QUICK: Step in place on right foot.
15–16	SLOW: Step to side on right foot, making ¼ turn left to Closed Position.	SLOW: Step to side on left foot, making ¼ turn right to Closed Position.
17	QUICK: Cross in back on left foot, making ⅛ turn left to Promenade Position.	QUICK: Cross in back on right foot, making ⅛ turn right to Promenade Position.
18	QUICK: Step in place on right foot.	QUICK: Step in place on left foot.
19–20	SLOW: Step forward on left foot, making ⅛ turn right to Closed Position.	SLOW: Step back on right foot, making ⅛ turn left to Closed Position.
21–24	QUICK-QUICK-SLOW: Final four counts of Basic Rumba Box.	QUICK-QUICK-SLOW: Final four counts of Basic Rumba Box.

Count 5

Count 6

Counts 7–8

Counts 9 and 17

Counts 10 and 18

Counts 11–12

Count 13

Count 14

Counts 15–16

Simple Wheel and Wrap-Around

2/2 ("cut") time
Recommended measures per minute:
  28–34
6 measures or 24 musical counts

COUNT	MAN'S PART	WOMAN'S PART
1–8	Complete Basic Rumba Box (Figure No. 1), on Count 7–8 stepping to side on right foot and making ¼ turn right as you remove right hand from partner's back and prepare to turn clockwise in a *wheel*, her right hand in your left.	Complete Basic Rumba Box (Figure No. 1), on Count 7–8 stepping forward on left foot as usual.
9–16	QUICK - QUICK - SLOW - QUICK - QUICK - SLOW: Beginning with left foot, take six steps backward to right (clockwise), covering approximately a half circle. Hands are at shoulder height.	QUICK - QUICK - SLOW - QUICK - QUICK - SLOW: Beginning with right foot, take six steps forward to right (clockwise), covering approximately a half circle — walking smoothly and with dignity.
17–24	Continue to lead partner in second half circle to her right while you do a neat *turning basic*, as follows: QUICK: Step to side on left foot. QUICK: Close right foot to left foot. SLOW: Step forward on left foot and begin ½ turn left (partner's hand is released as it passes under your right arm, leaving your left hand at your right hip). QUICK: Step to side on right foot. QUICK: Close left foot to right foot. SLOW: Step back on right foot and complete your turn left to resume Closed Position (the exact degree of your turn will depend on position of partner on final count).	QUICK - QUICK - SLOW - QUICK - QUICK - SLOW: Repeat Counts 9 through 16 exactly to face partner in Closed Position on the final count.

Counts 7–8

Count 9

Count 10

Counts 11–12

Count 17

Count 18

Counts 19–20

Count 21

Count 22

Cross-Body Lead to Cross Rocks to Solo Turns

2/2 ("cut") time

Recommended measures per minute:
28–34

6 measures or 24 musical counts

COUNT	MAN'S PART	WOMAN'S PART
1–8	Complete Basic Rumba Box (Figure No. 1) with right foot *toeing in* on Count 7–8.	Complete Basic Rumba Box (Figure No. 1).
9	QUICK: Step to side on left foot, making ¼ turn left as you lead partner across to your left (a *cross-body lead*, right hand at her back and left hand-hold lowered with thumb pointing across).	QUICK: Step forward on right foot.
10	QUICK: Close right foot to left foot, continuing to lead partner across.	QUICK: Step forward on left foot.
11–12	SLOW: Step forward diagonally on left foot to face partner and lead her into ¾ turn left to Open Counter Promenade Position (her right hand in your left).	SLOW: Step forward on right foot, making ¾ turn left into Open Counter Promenade Position.
13–16	QUICK-QUICK-SLOW: Take three steps forward (right foot, left foot, right foot).	QUICK-QUICK-SLOW: Take three steps forward (left foot, right foot, left foot).
17	QUICK: Rock forward on left foot.	QUICK: Rock forward on right foot.
18	QUICK: Replace weight on right foot.	QUICK: Replace weight on left foot.
19–20	SLOW: Step to side on left foot, releasing hand-hold and turning to face partner and lead her into *solo turn* to her right (your right hand makes lead contact to back of her left hand).	SLOW: Step to side on right foot, turning to face partner (remember to keep free arm raised at all times).
21–24	QUICK-QUICK-SLOW: Keeping left foot in one place, take three turning steps to left (right foot, left foot, right foot) to resume Closed Position as you both complete your solo turns.	QUICK-QUICK-SLOW: Keeping right foot in one place, take three turning steps to right (left foot, right foot, left foot) to return to Closed Position.

Count 9

Count 10

Counts 11–12

Counts 15–16

Count 17

Counts 19–20

Count 21

Count 22

Counts 23–24

Tea For Two Cha Cha

Music by
Vincent Youmans

Words by
Irving Caesar

Arranged by
Norval Gallant

PIANO SOLO

When Performing This Composition Kindly Give All Program Credits To
HARMS INC.
NEW YORK, N. Y.

Printed in U.S.A.

The Cha-cha

¢ 𝅘𝅥 𝅘𝅥 𝅘𝅥 𝅘𝅥𝅮𝅘𝅥𝅮 | 𝅘𝅥 𝅘𝅥 𝅘𝅥 𝅘𝅥𝅮𝅘𝅥𝅮 |

The cha-cha is written in "cut" time with a four-count rhythm correspond-
ing to three quarter notes and two eighth notes. It is the most popular of
the Latin dances today despite the fact that many beginners require a good
deal of practice to become accustomed to its catchy rhythm. The timing of
the *triple* (the *cha-cha-cha*), however, is identical to that of the *Triple Lindy:*
double-quick (one-half count), *double-quick* (one-half count), *quick* (one
count).

Since the two eighth notes come at the end of the measure, proper
phrasing requires a *lead-in* to put the *cha-cha-cha* on the "4 and 1" count
(that is, the fourth count of one measure and the first count of the next
measure). Although we have provided each figure in this chapter with
lead-in steps (Counts 1–5), the lead-in is to be used only at the start of the
dance; the couple then proceeds from one figure to another without
repeating the lead-in. For example, if the dance is begun with the Side
Basic or *cross rocks* (Figure No. 2), the figure should be done exactly as it is
described in the text. If, on the other hand, the dance has begun with the
Passing Basic (Figure No. 1), the man removes his right hand from the
woman's back on Count 12–13 (which corresponds to Count 4–5 of the
lead-in) and follows his *cha-cha-cha* to the right with Count 6 of the Side
Basic figure.

In cha-cha as in rumba, shoulders remain quiet and free arms are kept at
about shoulder level with palms down. All steps are taken on the flat of the
foot with the exception of the back step, which is taken on the ball of the
foot with weight kept well forward. Forward steps are taken with weight
held back.

Cha-Cha Figure No. 1
Passing Basic (with Lead-in)

2/2 ("cut") time
Recommended measures per minute:
26–32
3¼ measures or 13 musical counts

COUNT	MAN'S PART	WOMAN'S PART
1	From Closed Position, step diagonally back on left foot.	Step diagonally forward on right foot.
2	Step back on ball of right foot.	Step forward on left foot.
3	Step in place on left foot.	Step in place on right foot.
4–5	*Cha-cha-cha* diagonally forward to right in a *chassé* (three short steps) as follows: Diagonally forward on right foot (½ count); closing left foot to right foot (½ count); diagonally forward on right foot (1 full count).	*Cha-cha-cha* diagonally back to left in a *chassé* (three short steps) as follows: Diagonally back on left foot (½ count); closing right foot to left foot (½ count); diagonally back on left foot (1 full count).
6	Step forward on left foot.	Step back on ball of right foot.
7	Step in place on right foot.	Step in place on left foot.
8–9	*Cha-cha-cha* diagonally back to left (left foot, right foot, left foot).	*Cha-cha-cha* diagonally forward to right (right foot, left foot, right foot).
10	Step back on ball of right foot.	Step forward on left foot.
11	Step in place on left foot.	Step in place on right foot.
12–13	*Cha-cha-cha* diagonally forward to right (right foot, left foot, right foot).	*Cha-cha-cha* diagonally back to left (left foot, right foot, left foot).

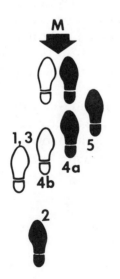

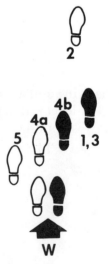

Count 1

Count 2

Count 3

Count 4 (a): *Cha-*

Count 4 (b): *Cha-*

Count 5: *Cha*

Cha-Cha Figure No. 2

Side Basic or "Cross Rocks"
(with Lead-in)

2/2 ("cut") time

Recommended measures per minute:
26–32

3¼ measures or 13 musical counts

COUNT	MAN'S PART	WOMAN'S PART
1	From Closed Position, step diagonally back on left foot as in Figure No. 1.	Step diagonally forward on right foot as in Figure No. 1.
2	Step back on right foot.	Step forward on left foot.
3	Step in place on left foot.	Step in place on right foot.
4–5	*Cha-cha-cha* to right (right foot, left foot, right foot), removing right hand from partner's back.	*Cha-cha-cha* to left (left foot, right foot, left foot).
6	Cross left foot in front of right foot, leading partner with left hand as you turn right and rock forward in Open Counter Promenade Position (free arm raised in "armchair" position).	Cross right foot in front of left foot, turning left, and rock forward in Open Counter Promenade Position (free arm raised in "armchair" position).
7	Replace weight on right foot, turning left to face partner.	Replace weight on left foot, turning right to face partner.
8–9	*Cha-cha-cha* to left (left foot, right foot, left foot), releasing partner's right hand as you take her left hand in your right.	*Cha-cha-cha* to right (right foot, left foot, right foot).
10	Cross right foot in front of left foot, leading partner with right hand as you turn left and rock forward in Open Promenade Position.	Cross left foot in front of right foot, turning right, and rock forward in Open Promenade Position.
11	Replace weight on left foot, turning right to face partner.	Replace weight on right foot, turning left to face partner.
12–13	*Cha-cha-cha* to right (right foot, left foot, right foot). At this point, you may repeat Counts 6–11 if you wish or simply resume Closed Position in preparation for the next figure.	*Cha-cha-cha* to left (left foot, right foot, left foot).

Count 4 (a)

Count 4 (b)

Count 5

Count 6

Count 7

Count 8 (a)

Count 8 (b)

Count 9

Count 10

Cha-Cha Figure No. 3
Cross Rocks to Arch Turn
for Woman

2/2 ("cut") time
Recommended measures per minute:
  26–32
3¼ measures or 13 musical counts

COUNT	MAN'S PART	WOMAN'S PART
1–9	Complete Counts 1–9 of the Side Basic with lead-in (Figure No. 2).	Same.
10	Rock back on right foot, raising left hand and turning partner's right hand in an *arch* over her head as your right hand on her back leads her into turn to her right.	Cross left foot in front of right foot (the first of five steps in a full turn to right).
11	Step in place on left foot as you continue turning partner to her right.	Step in place on right foot, continuing to turn right.
12–13	*Cha-cha-cha* in place (right foot, left foot, right foot) as you lead partner to complete her full turn to right and resume Closed Position.	*Cha-cha-cha* in place (left foot, right foot, left foot), completing full turn right to face partner in Closed Position.

Count 10

Count 11

Count 12 (a)

Cha-Cha Figure No. 4
Cross Rocks to Solo Turns

2/2 ("cut") time
Recommended measures per minute:
26–32
3¼ measures or 13 musical counts

COUNT	MAN'S PART	WOMAN'S PART
1–9	Complete Counts 1–9 of the Side Basic with lead-in (Figure No. 2).	Same.
10	Cross right foot in front of left foot, beginning to turn to left and releasing partner's left hand with strong lead into solo turn to her right.	Cross left foot in front of right foot, beginning a full turn to right (to be completed in five steps).
11	Step in place on left foot, continuing to turn to left.	Step in place on right foot, continuing to turn to right.
12–13	*Cha-cha-cha* in place (right foot, left foot, right foot), completing full turn left to face partner in Closed Position.	*Cha-cha-cha* in place (left foot, right foot, left foot), completing full turn right to face partner in Closed Position.

Count 10

Count 11

Count 12 (a)

Count 12 (b)

Count 13

2/2 ("cut") time
Recommended measures per minute:
26–32
5¼ measures or 21 musical counts

COUNT	MAN'S PART	WOMAN'S PART
1–5	Complete Counts 1–5 of Passing Basic with lead-in (Figure No. 1), assuming Challenge Position on Count 5.	Complete Counts 1–5 of Passing Basic with lead-in (Figure No. 1).
6	Step forward on left foot, beginning ½ turn to right (to be completed in two steps).	Rock back on right foot.
7	Step in place on right foot, completing turn to right with back to partner.	Replace weight on left foot.
8–9	*Cha-cha-cha* forward (left foot, right foot, left foot).	*Cha-cha-cha* forward (right foot, left foot, right foot), following partner.
10	Step forward on right foot, beginning ½ turn to left (to be completed in two steps).	Step forward on left foot, beginning ½ turn to right (to be completed in two steps).
11	Step in place on left foot, completing turn to left.	Step in place on right foot, completing turn to right with back to partner.
12–13	*Cha-cha-cha* forward (right foot, left foot, right foot), following partner.	*Cha-cha-cha* forward (left foot, right foot, left foot.)
14	Step forward on left foot (*or* repeat Counts 6–13 at this point).	Step forward on right foot, beginning ½ turn to left.
15	Step in place on right foot.	Step in place on left foot, completing turn to left to face partner.
16–17	*Cha-cha-cha* directly back (left foot, right foot, left foot) to resume Closed Position.	*Cha-cha-cha* directly forward (right foot, left foot, right foot) to resume Closed Position.
18–21	Complete Counts 10–13 of the Passing Basic (Figure No. 1), ending with weight on right foot in preparation for the next figure.	Complete Counts 10–13 of the Passing Basic (Figure No. 1), ending with weight on left foot in preparation for the next figure.

Count 5

Count 6

Count 7

Count 9

Count 10

Count 11

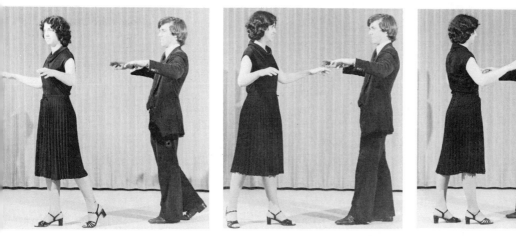

Count 14   Count 15   Count 17

Cha-Cha Figure No. 6
Breakaway to Cuddles

2/2 ("cut") time
Recommended measures per minute:
26–32
7¼ measures or 29 musical counts

COUNT	MAN'S PART	WOMAN'S PART
1–11	Complete Counts 1–11 of Passing Basic with lead-in (Figure No. 1), removing hand from partner's back on Count 11.	Complete Counts 1–11 of Passing Basic with lead-in (Figure No. 1).
12–13	*Cha-cha-cha* to right (right foot, left foot, right foot), lowering left hand to lead partner to Open Break Position and taking her right hand in your right.	*Cha-cha-cha* diagonally back to left (left foot, right foot, left foot) to Open Break Position.
14	Rock back on left foot.	Rock back on right foot.
15	Replace weight on right foot.	Replace weight on left foot.
16–17	*Cha-cha-cha* in place (left foot, right foot, left foot), leading partner in ½ turn left to Cuddle Position (your right arm across her back, right hand holding her right hand and left hand holding her left at shoulder level).	*Cha-cha-cha* in ½ turn left (right foot, left foot, right foot) to Cuddle Position at partner's right side.
18	Rock back on right (inside) foot.	Rock back on left (inside) foot.
19	Replace weight on left foot.	Replace weight on right foot.
20–21	*Cha-cha-cha* in place (right foot, left foot, right foot) as you lead partner (her back to you) to your left side.	*Cha-cha-cha* to left (left foot, right foot, left foot) as you move across partner to Cuddle Position at his left side.
22	Rock back on left (inside) foot.	Rock back on right (inside) foot.
23	Replace weight on right foot.	Replace weight on left foot.
24–25	*Cha-cha-cha* in place (left foot, right foot, left foot) as you lead partner across to your right side.	*Cha-cha-cha* to right (right foot, left foot, right foot) as you move across partner to Cuddle Position at his right side.
26	Rock back on right (inside) foot.	Rock back on left (inside) foot.
27	Replace weight on left foot.	Replace weight on right foot.
28–29	*Cha-cha-cha* forward (right foot, left foot, right foot) as left hand leads partner in ½ turn right to resume Closed Position.	*Cha-cha-cha* in ½ turn right (left foot, right foot, left foot) to face partner and resume Closed Position.

Count 12 (a)   Count 13   Count 14

Count 16 (a)   Count 17   Count 18

Count 20 (a)   Count 21   Count 22

THEY WERE DOIN' THE MAMBO

Words and Music by SONNY BURKE and DON RAYE

Featured by
VAUGHN MONROE
AND HIS ORCHESTRA

MAYFAIR MUSIC CORP.

35 West 51st Street   New York 19, N. Y.

The Mambo

The mambo is written in "cut" time with a four-count rhythm correspond-ing to four quarter notes. The primary accent is on the second count of the measure, and there is a secondary accent on the fourth count of the measure. Syncopation is often achieved by tying an accented note to the following weak note, thereby providing a jerky staccato effect.

Mambo is a fast dance in *quick-quick-slow* rhythm, with the *slow* corre-sponding to the "4 and 1" count (fourth count of one measure and first count of the next). This is similar to cha-cha, except that the triple (*cha-cha-cha*) becomes step-*hold*. As in cha-cha, knees are soft and all steps except back steps are on the flat of the foot; weight is held forward on back steps and held back on forward steps. Many figures of the two dances are interchangeable.

A lead-in is considered optional in mambo and is not included in the figures that follow. Proper phrasing can be achieved easily if the dance is started on the sharply accented second count of a measure — the man stepping forward on his left foot and the woman back on her right. Although it is somewhat more difficult to begin dancing on the weak first count of a mambo measure, the optional lead-in is identical with the one used in cha-cha figures (Counts 1–5), except that Count 4–5 becomes a step-*hold*. To be consistent with the figures in cha-cha, the first step in each mambo figure is commonly Count 6, the strong second count of the second measure of music.

Passing Basic (Without Lead-in)

2/2 ("cut") time
Recommended measures per minute: 34–48
2 measures or 8 musical counts

COUNT	MAN'S PART	WOMAN'S PART
6	QUICK (staccato): From Closed Position, on the sharply accented second beat of a measure, step forward on left foot.	QUICK (staccato): Step back on ball of right foot.
7	QUICK (staccato): Step in place on right foot.	QUICK (staccato): Step in place on left foot.
8–9	SLOW: Take a small step diagonally back on left foot (staccato) and *hold*.	SLOW: Take a small step diagonally forward on right foot (staccato) and *hold*.
10	QUICK (staccato): Step back on ball of right foot.	QUICK (staccato): Step forward on left foot.
11	QUICK (staccato): Step in place on left foot.	QUICK (staccato): Step in place on right foot.
12–13	SLOW: Take a small step diagonally forward on right foot (staccato) and *hold*.	SLOW: Take a small step diagonally back on left foot (staccato) and *hold*.

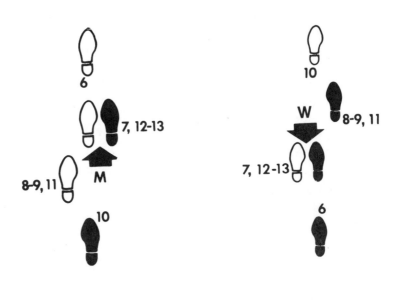

Count 6

Count 7

Counts 8–9

Count 10

Count 11

Counts 12–13

2/2 ("cut") time
Recommended measures per minute:
34–48
4 measures or 16 musical counts

COUNT	MAN'S PART	WOMAN'S PART
6–13	Complete all counts of Passing Basic (Figure No. 1), on Count 12–13 closing right foot to left foot and removing right hand from partner's back.	Complete all counts of Passing Basic (Figure No. 1).
14	QUICK: Step back on left foot (the first of three steps in a *commando*).	QUICK: Step back on right foot.
15	QUICK: Step in place on right foot.	QUICK: Step in place on left foot.
16–17	SLOW: Close left foot to right foot, raising left hand and turning partner's right hand in an *arch* over her head as your right hand on her back leads her into full turn to her right (to be completed in the next three steps).	SLOW: Step forward on right foot, beginning to turn right (the first of four steps in a full turn to right).
18	QUICK: Step back on right foot in a second *commando*, continuing to turn partner to her right.	QUICK: Step forward on left foot as you continue to turn right.
19	QUICK: Step in place on left foot as you continue to turn partner.	QUICK: Step in place on right foot as you continue to turn right.
20–21	SLOW: Close right foot to left foot as you lead partner to complete her full turn and resume Closed Position.	SLOW: Step forward on left foot, completing full turn to face partner in Closed Position.

Counts 12–13   Count 14   Count 15

Counts 16–17   Count 18

Count 19   Counts 20–21

2/2 ("cut") time
Recommended measures per minute:
34–48
4 measures or 16 musical counts

COUNT	MAN'S PART	WOMAN'S PART
6–13	Complete all counts of Passing Basic (Figure No. 1), on Count 12–13 closing right foot to left foot and removing right hand from partner's back.	Complete all counts of Passing Basic (Figure No. 1).
14	QUICK: Step back on left foot into Open Break Position.	QUICK: Step back on right foot into Open Break Position.
15	QUICK: Step in place on right foot.	QUICK: Step in place on left foot.
16–17	SLOW: Step diagonally forward on left foot, beginning to turn left (the first of four steps in a full turn) as you lead partner with your left hand at waist level into full turn to her right — and *release*.	SLOW: Step diagonally forward on right foot, beginning to turn right (the first of four steps in a full turn).
18	QUICK: Step forward on right foot as you continue to turn to left.	QUICK: Step forward on left foot as you continue to turn to right.
19	QUICK: Step in place on left foot as you continue to turn to left.	QUICK: Step in place on right foot as you continue to turn to right.
20-21	SLOW: Step forward on right foot, completing full turn to face partner and resume Closed Position.	SLOW: Step forward on left foot, completing full turn to face partner in Closed Position.

Counts 12–13   Count 14   Count 15

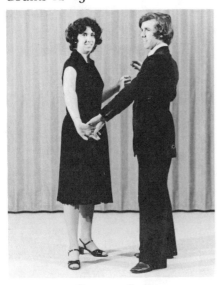

Counts 16–17   Count 18

Count 19   Counts 20–21

Mambo Figure No. 4
Promenade Twist

2/2 ("cut") time
Recommended measures per minute:
34–48
4 measures or 16 musical counts

COUNT	MAN'S PART	WOMAN'S PART
6–13	Complete all counts of Passing Basic (Figure No. 1), on Count 12–13 stepping to side on right foot.	Complete all counts of Passing Basic (Figure No. 1), on Count 12–13 stepping to side on left foot.
14	QUICK: Cross left foot in back of right foot, opening into Promenade Position.	QUICK: Cross right foot in back of left foot, opening into Promenade Position.
15	QUICK: Replace weight on right foot.	QUICK: Replace weight on left foot.
16–17	SLOW: Close left foot to right foot, turning right into Closed Position.	SLOW: Close right foot to left foot, turning left into Closed Position.
18	QUICK: Swiveling to Promenade Position on *left* foot, cross right foot in front of left foot and transfer weight.	QUICK: Swiveling to Promenade Position on *right* foot, cross left foot in front of right foot and transfer weight.
19	QUICK: Step to side on left foot, turning right to face partner.	QUICK: Step to side on right foot, turning left to face partner.
20–21	SLOW: Close right foot to left foot in Closed Position.	SLOW: Close left foot to right foot in Closed Position.

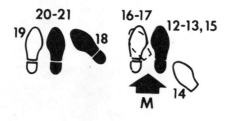

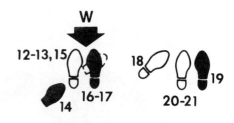

Counts 12–13   Count 14   Count 15

Counts 16–17   Count 18

Count 19   Counts 20–21

Mambo Figure No. 5
Swivel Basic

2/2 ("cut") time
Recommended measures per minute:
34–48
4 measures or 16 musical counts

COUNT	MAN'S PART	WOMAN'S PART
6–13	Complete all counts of Passing Basic (Figure No. 1).	Same.
14	QUICK: Step forward on left foot, turning left into Right Outside Position.	QUICK: Step back on right foot, turning left into Right Outside Position.
15	QUICK: Step in place on right foot.	QUICK: Step in place on left foot.
16–17	SLOW: Step back on left foot, leading partner forward and into ¼ turn to her right (so that she faces your right side).	SLOW: Step forward on right foot and swivel in ¼ turn right.
18	QUICK: Step back on right foot as you lead partner across in front of you.	QUICK: Cross left foot in front of right foot, swiveling to left as you step in front of partner to face him.
19	QUICK: Step in place on left foot and resume Closed Position.	QUICK: Step to side on right foot.
20–21	SLOW: Step forward on right foot.	SLOW: Step back on left foot.

Count 14

Count 15

Counts 16–17

Count 18

Count 19

Counts 20–21

The Tango

$$\frac{4}{4} \; \quad | \quad | \quad$$

Originally written in 2/4 time, today's tango is usually in 4/4 time. It is a graceful progressive dance with a basic rhythm of *slow-slow-quick-quick-slow*. The hold in tango is unique, with partners in close contact and "no daylight" between them. The man's right arm is farther around the woman and his left arm is closer to his body. Knees are flexed more than in any other ballroom dance and remain so throughout — with no rise-and-fall. Tango is a staccato dance. The stealthy effect achieved by many tango dancers results from holding every *slow* step until the last possible moment before moving the other foot.

In tango, there are three characteristic movements. In the tango *draw*, the ball of the foot is slowly drawn across the floor to the supporting foot without a change of weight. The *corté* is a stop and change of direction forward or backward (Figure No. 3). The *fan* is a half-turn done on the ball of one foot with the free foot held directly behind it (Figure No. 4).

The track in tango is a wide arc to the left. This is done with *Contrary Body Movement*, defined as the action of turning the opposite hip and shoulder toward the direction of the moving leg, and with *Contrary Body Movement Position*, a position attained when either foot is placed across the front or back of the body without the body turning. (Figure skaters will recognize this concept; in doing a Figure Eight, it is necessary at all times to keep the shoulders and hips perpendicular to the circle being traced.) Although you will find that the tango figures in this book include italicized directions for *CBM* and *CBMP*, they should not be of concern to you until you can perform the basic figures with ease.

Tango Figure No. 1
Forward Basic

4/4 time
Recommended measures per minute:
26–30
2 measures or 8 musical counts

COUNT	MAN'S PART	WOMAN'S PART
	It is strongly suggested that italicized notes regarding the advanced concepts of *Contrary Body Movement (CBM)* and *Contrary Body Movement Position (CBMP)* be ignored until you are able to perform a few of the basic tango figures easily.	
1–2	SLOW: From Closed Position with right hand farther around on partner's back and "no daylight" between you, step forward on left foot *in CBMP, right shoulder and hip turned toward the moving leg and thighs locked; travel is in a wide arc to the left.*	SLOW: Step back on right foot *in CBMP with left hip and shoulder in advance of right and thighs locked.*
3–4	SLOW: Step forward on right foot *with thighs unlocked, right shoulder and hip continuing in advance of left.*	SLOW: Step back on left foot *with thighs unlocked, left hip and shoulder continuing in advance of right.*
5	QUICK: Step forward on left foot *with thighs locked, right shoulder and hip in advance of left.*	QUICK: Step back on right foot *with left hip and shoulder in advance of right and thighs locked.*
6	QUICK: Step to side on right foot.	QUICK: Step to side on left foot.
7–8	SLOW: Draw left foot across floor to right foot without transferring weight, in preparation for next figure.	SLOW: Draw right foot across floor to left foot without transferring weight, in preparation for next figure.

7-8   6

5

3-4

1-2

Counts 1–2

Counts 3–4

Count 5

Count 6

M

W

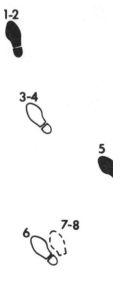

1-2

3-4

5

6   7-8

Counts 7–8

Tango Figure No. 2
Outside Basic

4/4 time
Recommended measures per minute:
26–30
2 measures or 8 musical counts

COUNT	MAN'S PART	WOMAN'S PART
1–2	SLOW: From Closed Position, step forward diagonally on left foot, preparing to go into Right Outside Position.	SLOW: Step diagonally back on right foot.
3–4	SLOW: Cross right foot in front of left foot as you step into Right Outside Position *with thighs locked in CBMP.*	SLOW: Cross left foot in back of right foot as you step into Right Outside Position *with thighs locked in CBMP.*
5	QUICK: Step forward on left foot into Closed Position.	QUICK: Step back on right foot.
6	QUICK: Step to side on right foot.	QUICK: Step to side on left foot.
7–8	SLOW: Draw left foot to right foot without transferring weight.	SLOW: Draw right foot to left foot without transferring weight.

Counts 1–2

Counts 3–4

Count 5

Tango Figure No. 3
Simple *Corté* to Tango Draw

4/4 time
Recommended measures per minute:
26–30
2 measures or 8 musical counts

COUNT	MAN'S PART	WOMAN'S PART
1–2	SLOW: With knee slightly more flexed, step back on left foot in a *corté*.	SLOW: With knee slightly more flexed, step forward on right foot in a *corté*.
3–4	SLOW: Replace weight on right foot.	SLOW: Replace weight on left foot.
5	QUICK: Step forward on left foot *with thighs locked in CBMP*.	QUICK: Step back on right foot *with thighs locked in CBMP*.
6	QUICK: Step to side on right foot.	QUICK: Step to side on left foot.
7–8	SLOW: Draw left foot to right foot without transferring weight.	SLOW: Draw right foot to left foot without transferring weight.

Counts 1–2   Counts 3–4   Count 5

Count 6   Counts 7–8

4/4 time

Recommended measures per minute: 26–30

3½ measures or 14 musical counts

COUNT	MAN'S PART	WOMAN'S PART
1–2	SLOW: From Closed Position, step to side on left foot, making turn left to Promenade Position.	SLOW: Step to side on right foot, making turn right to Promenade Position.
3–4	SLOW: Cross right foot in front of left foot *with thighs locked in CBMP*.	SLOW: Cross left foot in front of right foot *with thighs locked in CBMP*.
5	QUICK: Rock forward on left foot.	QUICK: Rock forward on right foot.
6	QUICK: Replace weight on right foot, leading partner to Right Outside Position.	QUICK: Replace weight on left foot, turning left to Right Outside Position.
7–8	SLOW: With knee slightly more flexed, step back on left foot in a *corté* as you lead partner in fan to her right.	SLOW: Step forward on right foot and fan (½ turn right) with left foot held directly behind right foot.
9–10	SLOW: Replace weight on right foot, now in Promenade Position.	SLOW: Step forward on left foot, now in Promenade Position.
11	QUICK: Step forward on left foot, bringing partner to Closed Position with a strong right hand lead.	QUICK: Step forward on right foot, making ½ turn left to Closed Position.
12	QUICK: Step to side on right foot.	QUICK: Step to side on left foot.
13–14	SLOW: Draw left foot to right foot without transferring weight.	SLOW: Draw right foot to left foot without transferring weight.

Counts 1–2   Counts 3–4   Count 5

Count 6   Counts 7–8

Counts 9–10   Counts 13–14

Tango Figure No. 5
Open Fan

4/4 time
Recommended measures per minute:
26–30
4 measures or 16 musical counts

COUNT	MAN'S PART	WOMAN'S PART
1–4	Complete first four counts of Fan for Woman (Figure No. 4).	Same.
5	QUICK: Step to side on left foot, making turn right to Closed Position and removing right hand from partner's back.	QUICK: Step to side on right foot, making turn left to Closed Position.
6	QUICK: Step to side on right foot, making turn right into Open Counter Promenade Position.	QUICK: Step to side on left foot, making turn left into Open Counter Promenade Position.
7–8	SLOW: Draw left foot to right foot without transferring weight.	SLOW: Draw right foot to left foot without transferring weight.
9–10	SLOW: Step diagonally forward on left foot and fan (½ turn left) with right foot held directly behind left foot, resuming Promenade Position with right hand on partner's back.	SLOW: Step diagonally forward on right foot and fan (½ turn right) with left foot held directly behind right foot, resuming Promenade Position.
11–12	SLOW: Step forward on right foot.	SLOW: Step forward on left foot.
13	QUICK: Step forward on left foot, bringing partner to Closed Position with a strong right hand lead.	QUICK: Step forward on right foot, making ½ turn left to Closed Position.
14	QUICK: Step to side on right foot.	QUICK: Step to side on left foot.
15–16	SLOW: Draw left foot to right foot without transferring weight.	SLOW: Draw right foot to left foot without transferring weight.

Counts 3–4   Count 5   Counts 7–8

Count 9   Count 10   Counts 11–12

Count 13   Count 14   Counts 15–16

Tango Figure No. 6

Left-Turning Rocks to Simple
Corté

4/4 time
Recommended measures per minute:
26–30
4 measures or 16 musical counts

COUNT	MAN'S PART	WOMAN'S PART
1–4	Complete first four counts of Forward Basic (Figure No. 1).	Same.
5	QUICK: Rock forward on left foot with body turning to left, *thighs locked in CBM.*	QUICK: Rock back on right foot with body turning to left, *thighs locked in CBM.*
6	QUICK: Rock back on right foot with body turning to left, *thighs locked.*	QUICK: Rock forward on left foot with body turning to left, *thighs locked.*
7–8	QUICK-QUICK: Repeat Counts 5 and 6.	QUICK-QUICK: Repeat Counts 5 and 6.
9–10	SLOW: With knee slightly more flexed, step back on left foot in a *corté.*	SLOW: With knee slightly more flexed, step forward on right foot in a *corté.*
11–12	SLOW: Replace weight on right foot.	SLOW: Replace weight on left foot.
13	QUICK: Step forward on left foot *with thighs locked.*	QUICK: Step back on right foot *with thighs locked.*
14	QUICK: Step to side on right foot.	QUICK: Step to side on left foot.
15–16	SLOW: Draw left foot to right foot without transferring weight.	SLOW: Draw right foot to left foot without transferring weight.

Count 5

Count 6

Count 7

Count 8

Counts 9–10

Counts 11–12

Count 13

Count 14

Counts 15–16

The Samba

The original Brazilian sambas were written in 2/4 time, but the dance we know today is almost always played in "cut" time with a syncopated pulsing beat. The rhythm consists of three steps to two counts of music, which many dancers call *step-and-cut*. Characteristics of the dance include *pendulum motion*, where the entire body sways opposite to the feet (step forward, sway back; step right, sway left and so forth), and continuous bending and straightening of the knees which adds to the samba's smooth lilting effect.

Because of the fast tempo, all steps in samba are fairly short. The basic footwork requires considerable practice before it can be done with precision and ease. The man takes a STEP forward on his left foot (¾ count), AND nearly closes his right foot to it, taking partial weight on the ball of the foot (¼ count), almost simultaneously closing the left foot to the right with a pulling action from the hip (the CUT) to take full weight for one count. The woman does the counterpart.

While samba is one of the more difficult ballroom dances, it is also one of the most enjoyable. The music is a challenge, and the dance is well worth the time and effort required to learn the basic movements. You will find that once you have mastered the basic steps in samba, its other figures will seem much easier.

Samba Figure No. 1
Brazilian Basic

2/2 ("cut") time
Recommended measures per minute:
50–60
2 measures or 4 musical counts

COUNT	MAN'S PART	WOMAN'S PART
	Basic samba movement (usually called a *step-and-cut*) when done as follows will result in the couple rocking back and forth in a pendulum motion.	
1	From Closed Position, STEP forward on left foot with knees flexed so that body tilts slightly back (¾ count),	STEP back on ball of right foot with knees almost straight so that body tilts slightly forward (¾ count),
	AND nearly close right foot to left foot, taking *partial* weight on ball of right foot — knees flexed (¼ count).	AND nearly close left foot to right foot, taking *partial* weight on ball of left foot — knees straight (¼ count).
2	CUT (or "pull") left foot to right foot, taking full weight — knees relaxed (one full count).	CUT (or "pull") right foot to left foot, taking full weight — knees relaxed (one full count).
3	STEP back on ball of right foot with knees almost straight so that body tilts slightly forward (¾ count),	STEP forward on left foot with knees flexed so that body tilts slightly back (¾ count),
	AND nearly close left foot to right foot, taking *partial* weight on ball of left foot — knees straight (¼ count).	AND nearly close right foot to left foot, taking *partial* weight on ball of right foot — knees flexed (¼ count).
4	CUT right foot to left foot, taking full weight — knees relaxed (one full count).	CUT left foot to right foot, taking full weight — knees relaxed (one full count).

After you have mastered the back-and-forth movement of samba you will find that this figure easily becomes a *turning basic* with a quarter turn left on the forward and back steps.

Count 1 (a): STEP

Count 1 (b): AND

Count 2: CUT

Count 3 (a): STEP

Count 3 (b): AND

Count 4: CUT

Samba Figure No. 2
Extended Basic

2/2 ("cut") time

Recommended measures per minute:
50–60

4 measures or 8 musical counts

COUNT	MAN'S PART	WOMAN'S PART
1	From Closed Position, STEP forward on left foot with knees flexed so that body tilts slightly back (¾ count), AND nearly close right foot to left foot, taking partial weight on ball of right foot — knees flexed (¼ count).	STEP back on ball of right foot with knees almost straight so that body tilts slightly forward (¾ count), AND nearly close left foot to right foot, taking partial weight on ball of left foot — knees straight (¼ count).
2	CUT left foot to right foot, taking full weight — knees relaxed (¾ count), AND take short step to side on ball of right foot, taking partial weight — knees flexed (¼ count).	CUT right foot to left foot, taking full weight — knees relaxed (¾ count), AND take short step to side on ball of left foot, taking partial weight — knees straight (¼ count).
3	CUT-AND: Repeat Count 2.	CUT-AND: Repeat Count 2.
4	CUT left foot to right foot, taking full weight — knees relaxed (one full count).	CUT right foot to left foot, taking full weight — knees relaxed (one full count).
5	STEP back on ball of right foot with knees almost straight so that body tilts slightly forward (¾ count), AND nearly close left foot to right foot, taking partial weight on ball of left foot — knees straight (¼ count).	STEP forward on left foot with knees flexed so that body tilts slightly back (¾ count), AND nearly close right foot to left foot, taking partial weight on ball of right foot — knees flexed (¼ count).
6	CUT right foot to left foot, taking full weight — knees relaxed (¾ count), AND take short step to side on ball of left foot, taking partial weight — knees straight (¼ count).	CUT left foot to right foot, taking full weight — knees relaxed (¾ count), AND take short step to side on ball of right foot taking partial weight — knees flexed (¼ count).
7	CUT-AND: Repeat Count 6.	CUT-AND: Repeat Count 6.
8	CUT right foot to left foot, taking full weight — knees relaxed (one full count).	CUT left foot to right foot, taking full weight — knees relaxed (one full count).

Count 1 (a)

Count 1 (b)

Count 2 (a)

Count 3 (b)

Count 4

Count 5 (a)

Count 5 (b)

Count 6 (a)

Count 8

Samba Figure No. 3
Samba Walk in Promenade

2/2 ("cut") time
Recommended measures per minute:
50–60
8 measures or 16 musical counts

COUNT	MAN'S PART	WOMAN'S PART
1	From Closed Position, STEP forward on left foot with knees flexed so that body tilts slightly back (¾ count), AND step to side on ball of right foot, turning left to Promenade Position (¼ count).	STEP back on ball of right foot with knees almost straight so that body tilts slightly forward (¾ count), AND step to side on ball of left foot turning right to Promenade Position (¼ count).
2	CUT left foot to right foot — knees flexed (one full count).	CUT right foot to left foot — knees flexed (one full count).
3	STEP forward on right (inside) foot — knees flexed (¾ count), AND step back about an inch on ball of left foot (¼ count).	STEP forward on left (inside) foot — knees flexed (¾ count), AND step back about an inch on ball of right foot (¼ count).
4	CUT or "pull" right foot back one or two inches — knees relaxed (one full count).	CUT or "pull" left foot back one or two inches — knees relaxed (one full count).
5	STEP forward on left (outside) foot — knees flexed (¾ count), AND step back about an inch on ball of right foot (¼ count).	STEP forward on right (outside) foot — knees flexed (¾ count), AND step back about an inch on ball of left foot (¼ count).
6	CUT or "pull" left foot back one or two inches — knees relaxed (one full count).	CUT or "pull" right foot back one or two inches — knees relaxed (one full count).
7–14	Repeat Counts 3 through 6 twice.	Repeat Counts 3 through 6 twice.
15	STEP forward on right (inside) foot — knees flexed (¾ count), AND step to side on ball of left foot, turning right into Closed Position (¼ count).	STEP forward on left (inside) foot — knees flexed (¾ count), AND step to side on ball of right foot, turning left into Closed Position (¼ count).
16	CUT right foot to left foot — knees relaxed (one full count).	CUT left foot to right foot — knees relaxed (one full count).

Count 1 (a)

Count 1 (b)

Count 2

Count 3 (a)

Count 4

Count 5 (a)

Count 6

Count 15 (a)

Count 15 (b)

Samba Figure No. 4
Boto Fogos

2/2 ("cut") time
Recommended measures per minute:
50–60
8 measures or 16 musical counts

COUNT	MAN'S PART	WOMAN'S PART
1–2	Complete first two counts of Samba Walk in Promenade (Figure No. 3), continuing with your basic samba movement.	Same.
3	STEP across on right foot in front of left foot (¾ count), AND nearly close left foot to right foot, beginning turn right into Counter Promenade Position (¼ count).	STEP across on left foot in front of right foot (¾ count), AND nearly close right foot to left foot, beginning turn left into Counter Promenade Position (¼ count).
4	CUT right foot to left foot, completing turn into Counter Promenade Position (one full count).	CUT left foot to right foot, completing turn into Counter Promenade Position (one full count).
5	STEP across on left foot in front of right foot (¾ count), AND nearly close right foot to left foot, beginning turn left into Promenade Position (¼ count).	STEP across on right foot in front of left foot (¾ count), AND nearly close left foot to right foot, beginning turn right into Promenade Position (¼ count).
6	CUT left foot to right foot, completing turn into Promenade Position (one full count).	CUT right foot to left foot, completing turn into Promenade Position (one full count).
7–14	Repeat Counts 3–6 twice.	Repeat Counts 3–6 twice.
15	STEP forward on right (inside) foot (¾ count), AND step to side on left foot, turning right into Closed Position (¼ count).	STEP forward on left (inside) foot (¾ count), AND step to side on right foot, turning left into Closed Position (¼ count).
16	CUT right foot to left foot (one full count).	CUT left foot to right foot (one full count).

Count 2

Count 3 (a)

Count 3 (b)

Count 4

Count 5 (a)

Count 5 (b)

Count 6

Count 15 (a)

Count 15 (b)

Samba Figure No. 5
Twinkles with Extended Basic

2/2 ("cut") time
Recommended measures per minute:
  50–60
8 measures or 16 musical counts

COUNT	MAN'S PART	WOMAN'S PART
1	From Closed Position, STEP forward on left foot, turning left into Right Outside Position (¾ count), AND nearly close right foot to left foot (¼ count).	STEP back on right foot, turning left into Right Outside Position (¾ count), AND nearly close left foot to right foot (¼ count).
2	CUT left foot to right foot (one full count).	CUT right foot to left foot (one full count).
3	STEP forward on right foot, turning right into Left Outside Position (¾ count), AND nearly close left foot to right foot (¼ count).	STEP back on left foot, turning right into Left Outside Position (¾ count), AND nearly close right foot to left foot (¼ count).
4	CUT right foot to left foot (one full count).	CUT left foot to right foot (one full count).
5	STEP forward on left foot, turning left into Closed Position (¾ count), AND nearly close right foot to left foot (¼ count).	STEP back on right foot, turning left into Closed Position (¾ count), AND nearly close left foot to right foot (¼ count).
6–8	CUT-AND-CUT-AND-*CUT*: Complete Counts 2–4 of Extended Basic (Figure No. 2), on final count turning left into Right Outside Position.	CUT-AND-CUT-AND-*CUT*: Complete Counts 2–4 of Extended Basic (Figure No. 2), on final count turning left into Right Outside Position.
9–10	STEP-AND-CUT: Repeat Counts 3 and 4.	STEP-AND-CUT: Repeat Counts 3 and 4.
11	STEP forward on left foot, turning left into Right Outside Position (¾ count), AND nearly close right foot to left foot (¼ count).	STEP back on right foot, turning left into Right Outside Position (¾ count), AND nearly close left foot to right foot (¼ count).
12	CUT left foot to right foot (one full count).	CUT right foot to left foot (one full count).
13	STEP forward on right foot, turning right into Closed Position (¾ count), AND nearly close left foot to right foot (¼ count).	STEP back on left foot, turning right into Closed Position (¾ count), AND nearly close right foot to left foot (¼ count).
14–16	CUT-AND-CUT-AND-*CUT*: Complete Counts 6–8 of Extended Basic (Figure No. 2).	CUT-AND-CUT-AND-*CUT*: Complete Counts 6–8 of Extended Basic (Figure No. 2).

Count 2

Count 3 (a)

Count 3 (b)

Count 4

Count 5 (a)

Count 5 (b)

Count 8

Count 11 (a)

Count 12

MEDITATION
(Meditacáo)

Music by **ANTONIO CARLOS JOBIM**
English Words by **NORMAN GIMBEL**
Original Words by **NEWTON MENDONCA**

$1.50

DUCHESS MUSIC CORPORATION
SOLE SELLING AGENT MCA MUSIC, A DIVISION OF MCA INC.
25 Deshon Drive, Melville, N.Y. 11746

US 513

The Bossa Nova

$$¢ \; \textstyle\textstyle\quad \mathord{\halfnote}\; \mathord{\quarternote}\; \mathord{\eighthnote}\;\big|\; \mathord{\halfnote}\; \mathord{\quarternote}\; \mathord{\eighthnote}\;\big|$$

The bossa nova is written in "cut" time with a four-count *slow-quick-quick* rhythm which is just the reverse of the *quick-quick-slow* pattern of American rumba. It is sometimes difficult for beginners to differentiate between the two dances. Like rumba, bossa nova is a spot dance with characteristic Cuban Motion, quiet shoulders, and flat feet. In the basic figures, travel is usually done on the *slow* counts, with the *quicks* used to adjust position and step in place.

Bossa nova tends to be fluid, sensuous, and more relaxed than rumba. Many adaptations are borrowed from other Latin dances, such as the Tango Adaptation (Figure No. 4) and the Samba Adaptation (Figure No. 5). With the ready availability of beautiful bossa nova music, it is somewhat surprising that this easy and thoroughly enjoyable dance is not more widely known.

Bossa Nova Figure No. 1
Side Basic

2/2 ("cut") time
Recommended measures per minute:
28–44
2 measures or 8 musical counts

COUNT	MAN'S PART	WOMAN'S PART
1–2	SLOW (relaxed, with shoulders level and knees soft, using Cuban Motion): From Closed Position, step to side on left foot.	SLOW (relaxed, with shoulders level and knees soft, using Cuban Motion): Step to side on right foot.
3	QUICK (but not staccato): Close right foot to left foot.	QUICK (but not staccato): Close left foot to right foot.
4	QUICK: Step in place on left foot.	QUICK: Step in place on right foot.
5–6	SLOW: Step to side on right foot.	SLOW: Step to side on left foot.
7	QUICK: Close left foot to right foot.	QUICK: Close right foot to left foot.
8	QUICK: Step in place on right foot.	QUICK: Step in place on left foot.

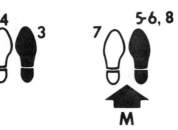

Counts 1–2

Count 3

Count 4

Counts 5–6

Count 7

Count 8

Bossa Nova Figure No. 2
Forward Basic

2/2 ("cut") time
Recommended measures per minute:
28–44
2 measures or 8 musical counts

COUNT	MAN'S PART	WOMAN'S PART
1–2	SLOW: From Closed Position, step forward on left foot.	SLOW: Step back on right foot.
3	QUICK: Close right foot to left foot.	QUICK: Close left foot to right foot.
4	QUICK: Step in place on left foot.	QUICK: Step in place on right foot.
5–6	SLOW: Step back on right foot.	SLOW: Step forward on left foot.
7	QUICK: Close left foot to right foot.	QUICK: Close right foot to left foot.
8	QUICK: Step in place on right foot.	QUICK: Step in place on left foot.

1-2,4   3

7   5-6, 8

M

W

5-6,8   7

3   1-2,4

Counts 1–2

Count 3

Count 4

Counts 5–6

Count 7

Count 8

Bossa Nova Figure No. 3
Away and Together

2/2 ("cut") time
Recommended measures per minute:
28–44
8 measures or 32 musical counts

COUNT	MAN'S PART	WOMAN'S PART
1–8	Complete all counts of Bossa Nova Forward Basic (Figure No. 2), on Count 7 making ⅛ turn right into Left Outside Position.	Same.
9–10	SLOW: Step back on left foot, making ⅛ turn left; raise left hand and with right hand lead partner in turn to her right (to side-by-side position).	SLOW: Step forward on right foot, turning right into side-by-side position.
11	QUICK: Close right foot to left foot.	QUICK: Close left foot to right foot.
12	QUICK: Step in place on left foot.	QUICK: Step in place on right foot.
13–14	SLOW: Step to side on right foot, *away* from partner.	SLOW: Step to side on left foot, *away* from partner.
15	QUICK: Close left foot to right foot.	QUICK: Close right foot to left foot.
16	QUICK: Step in place on right foot.	QUICK: Step in place on left foot.
17–18	SLOW: Step to side on left foot, *toward* partner.	SLOW: Step to side on right foot, *toward* partner.
19	QUICK: Close right foot to left foot.	QUICK: Close left foot to right foot.
20	QUICK: Step in place on left foot.	QUICK: Step in place on right foot.
21–24	Repeat Counts 13–16 exactly.	Repeat Counts 13–16 exactly.
25–26	SLOW: Step to side on left foot and raise left hand as you turn partner to her left into Closed Position.	SLOW: Step diagonally to side on right foot, making ½ turn left to face partner in Closed Position.
27	QUICK: Close right foot to left foot.	QUICK: Close left foot to right foot.
28	QUICK: Step in place on left foot.	QUICK: Step in place on right foot.
29–32	SLOW-QUICK-QUICK: Final four counts of Bossa Nova Side Basic (Figure No. 1).	SLOW-QUICK-QUICK: Final four counts of Bossa Nova Side Basic.

Count 8

Counts 9–10

Count 11

Count 12

Counts 13–14

Count 15

Counts 17–18

Counts 25–26

Count 27

Bossa Nova Figure No. 4
The Tango Adaptation

2/2 ("cut") time
Recommended measures per minute: 28–44
6 measures or 24 musical counts

COUNT	MAN'S PART	WOMAN'S PART
1–8	Complete all counts of Bossa Nova Forward Basic (Figure No. 2), on Count 7 making turn left into Right Outside Position.	Same.
9–10	SLOW: Step back on left foot as you *begin* to lead partner into ½ turn to her right (to be completed in next two counts).	SLOW: Step forward on right foot and *begin* ½ turn right (to be completed in the next two counts).
11	QUICK: Close right foot to left foot as you continue to turn partner.	QUICK: Close left foot to right foot as you continue turning right.
12	QUICK: Step in place on left foot as partner completes turn right into side-by-side position.	QUICK: Step in place on right foot as you complete turn right into side-by-side position.
13–14	SLOW: Step forward on right foot as you *begin* to lead partner into ½ turn to her left (to be completed in next two counts).	SLOW: Step forward on left foot and *begin* ½ turn left (to be completed in the next two counts).
15	QUICK: Close left foot to right foot as you continue to turn partner.	QUICK: Close right foot to left foot as you continue turning left.
16	QUICK: Step in place on right foot as partner completes turn left into Right Outside Position.	QUICK: Step in place on left foot as you complete turn left into Right Outside Position.
17–20	Repeat Counts 9–12 exactly.	Repeat Counts 9–12 exactly.
21–22	SLOW: Step forward on right foot and lead partner firmly into rapid 1½ turns to her left (to be completed in next two counts).	SLOW: Step forward on left foot and *begin* rapid 1½ turns left (to be completed in next two counts).
23	QUICK: Close left foot to right foot as you continue to turn partner.	QUICK: Close right foot to left foot as you continue turning left.
24	QUICK: Step in place on right foot as you bring partner into Closed Position.	QUICK: Step in place on left foot as you complete turn to face partner in Closed Position.

Count 8

Counts 9–10

Count 11

Count 12

Counts 13–14

Count 16

Counts 21–22

Count 23

Count 24

Bossa Nova Figure No. 5
The Samba Adaptation

2/2 ("cut") time
Recommended measures per minute:
28–44
6 measures or 24 musical counts

COUNT	MAN'S PART	WOMAN'S PART
1–4	Complete first four counts of Bossa Nova Forward Basic (Figure No. 2).	Same.
5–6	SLOW: Step to side on right foot, opening into Promenade Position.	SLOW: Step to side on left foot, opening into Promenade Position.
7	QUICK: Close left foot to right foot.	QUICK: Close right foot to left foot.
8	QUICK: Step in place on right foot.	QUICK: Step in place on left foot.
9–10	SLOW: Rock forward on left foot.	SLOW: Rock forward on right foot.
11	QUICK: Rock back on ball of right foot.	QUICK: Rock back on ball of left foot.
12	QUICK: Replace weight on left foot.	QUICK: Replace weight on right foot.
13–14	SLOW: Rock forward on right foot.	SLOW: Rock forward on left foot.
15	QUICK: Rock back on ball of left foot.	QUICK: Rock back on ball of right foot.
16	QUICK: Replace weight on right foot.	QUICK: Replace weight on left foot.
17–18	SLOW: Step to side on left foot, turning right into Closed Position.	SLOW: Step to side on right foot, turning left into Closed Position.
19	QUICK: Close right foot to left foot.	QUICK: Close left foot to right foot.
20	QUICK: Step in place on left foot.	QUICK: Step in place on right foot.
21–24	SLOW-QUICK-QUICK: Final four counts of Bossa Nova Side Basic (Figure No. 1).	SLOW-QUICK-QUICK: Final four counts of Bossa Nova Side Basic (Figure No. 1).

Counts 5–6

Count 8

Counts 9–10

Count 11

Counts 13–14

Count 15

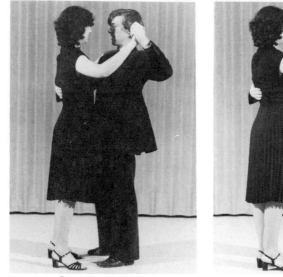

Counts 17–18

Count 19

The Merengue

The merengue was originally written in 2/4 time but is now usually in "cut" time. It is similar to a march, except that every other measure is syncopated. From the musical notation above, you can see that merengue consists of one measure identical to samba music followed by a measure similar to a fast march. The first beat of each syncopated measure is strongly accented, and there is a secondary accent on the first beat of the next measure. Merengue is danced to a two-count *quick-quick* rhythm.

The characteristic feature of merengue is its *side basic* or *chassé*. A controlled Cuban Motion is used with small steps, and the hip movement is more subtle than in other Latin dances. There is little or no movement of the upper body, although some dancers add a deep flexing of the man's right knee (woman's left) and a slight sideward dip of the man's left shoulder (woman's right) on the strong first beat of each syncopated measure (Counts 1 and 5).

Merengue is a very easy dance to learn, and many of its figures are quite simple. It may be done in a light and casual manner or with sophisticated style. This "fun" dance and its fascinating music belong on every dance program.

Merengue Figure No. 1
Basic Chassé

2/2 ("cut") time
Recommended measures per minute:
  56–68
2 measures or 4 musical counts

COUNT	MAN'S PART	WOMAN'S PART
1	From Closed Position (using your Cuban Motion), take a small step to side on left foot; transfer weight and then straighten left leg until you "sit" on left hip. The movement remains subtle and must not be exaggerated with the more sharply accented beat of merengue music.	Using your Cuban Motion, take a small step to side on right foot; transfer weight and then straighten right leg until you "sit" on right hip. For you also the hip movement must remain very subtle. Remember that hips move only through knee action.
2	Close right foot to left foot; transfer weight and straighten right leg until you "sit" on right hip.	Close left foot to right foot; transfer weight and straighten left leg until you "sit" on left hip.
3	Take small step to side on left foot, continuing Cuban Motion throughout.	Take small step to side on right foot, continuing Cuban Motion throughout.
4	Close right foot to left foot.	Close left foot to right foot.

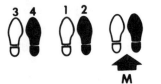

Count 1

Count 2

A simple variation of the merengue chassé is called "The Stair" for obvious reasons: the man takes a step forward on Count 3 while the woman steps back.

Merengue Figure No. 2
Quarter Turns

2/2 ("cut") time
Recommended measures per minute:
  56–68
2 measures or 4 musical counts

COUNT	MAN'S PART	WOMAN'S PART
1	From Closed Position, step forward on left foot.	Step back on right foot.
2	Step in place on right foot.	Step in place on left foot.
3	Step to side on left foot, making ¼ turn left.	Step to side on right foot, making ¼ turn left.
4	Close right foot to left foot.	Close left foot to right foot.

Count 1

Count 2

Count 3

Count 4

Merengue Figure No. 3
Grapevine to Left

2/2 ("cut") time
Recommended measures per minute:
  56–68
4 measures or 8 musical counts

COUNT	MAN'S PART	WOMAN'S PART
1	From Closed Position, with weight held back, cross left foot in back of right foot (opening into Promenade Position).	With weight held back, cross right foot in back of left foot (opening into Promenade Position).
2	Replace weight on right foot.	Replace weight on left foot.
3	Step to side on left foot (into Closed Position).	Step to side on right foot (into Closed Position).
4	Cross right foot in back of left foot (into Counter Promenade Position).	Cross left foot in back of right foot (into Counter Promenade Position).
5	Step to side on left foot (into Closed Position).	Step to side on right foot (into Closed Position).
6	Cross right foot in front of left foot (into Promenade Position).	Cross left foot in front of right foot (into Promenade Position).
7	Step to side on left foot (into Closed Position).	Step to side on right foot (into Closed Position).
8	Close right foot to left foot.	Close left foot to right foot.

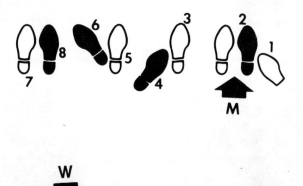

Count 1

Count 2

Count 3

Count 4

Count 5

Count 6

Count 7

Count 8

Merengue Figure No. 4
Away and Together

2/2 ("cut") time
Recommended measures per minute:
56–68
10 measures or 20 musical counts

COUNT	MAN'S PART	WOMAN'S PART
1–2	From Closed Position, step to side on left foot in a basic merengue *chassé* (the first of three steps to left); close right foot to left foot.	Step to side on right foot in a basic merengue *chassé* (the first of seven steps to right); close left foot to right foot.
3–4	Step to side on left foot; *tap* right foot beside left foot.	Step to side on right foot; close left foot to right foot.
5–6	Step to side on right foot (the first of three steps to right), dropping partner's right hand and taking her left hand in your left; close left foot to right foot.	Step to side on right foot; close left foot to right foot.
7–8	Step to side on right foot; *tap* left foot beside right foot.	Step to side on right foot; *tap* left foot beside right foot.
9–10	Step to side on left foot (the first of seven steps to left); close right foot to left foot.	Step to side on left foot (the first of seven steps to left); close right foot to left foot.
11–12	Step to side on left foot; close right foot to left foot, dropping partner's left hand and taking her right hand in your right.	Step to side on left foot; close right foot to left foot.
13–14	Step to side on left foot; close right foot to left foot.	Step to side on left foot; close right foot to left foot.
15–16	Step to side on left foot; *tap* right foot beside left foot.	Step to side on left foot; *tap* right foot beside left foot.
17–18	Step to side on right foot (the first of three steps to right); close left foot to right foot.	Step to side on right foot (the first of four steps to right); close left foot to right foot.
19–20	Step to side on right foot; *tap* left foot beside right foot, reversing your direction and resuming Closed Position.	Step to side on right foot; close left foot to right foot as you resume Closed Position.

Count 4

Count 5

Count 6

Count 7

Count 8

Count 9

Count 10

Count 11

Count 12

Merengue Figure No. 5

Left Spot Turn to Breakaway to Wheel and Arch

2/2 ("cut") time
Recommended measures per minute:
56–68
8 measures or 16 musical counts

COUNT	MAN'S PART	WOMAN'S PART
1	From Closed Position, step forward on left foot with heel in front of right toe, body beginning to turn to left.	Step diagonally back on right foot with right toe turning in slightly, body beginning to turn to left.
2	Step to side on right foot, still turning to left.	Step back on left foot with instep behind heel of right foot, still turning to left.
3–4	Repeat Counts 1 and 2.	Repeat Counts 1 and 2.
5	Step forward on left foot, removing right hand from partner's back.	Step back on right foot.
6	Replace weight on right foot, lowering left hand-hold to lead partner away from you to Open Break Position.	Step back on left foot into Open Break Position.
7	Close left foot to right foot.	Close right foot to left foot.
8	Step in place on right foot.	Step in place on left foot.
9–12	Take four steps forward (left foot, right foot, left foot, right foot), circling to right in Right Outside Position.	Take four steps forward (right foot, left foot, right foot, left foot), circling to right in Right Outside Position.
13	Take small step to side on left foot, raising left hand and turning partner's right hand over her head in an *arch* as your right hand on her back leads her into ½ turn to her right.	Step forward on right foot, making a rapid ½ turn right. This is the first step of a full turn to right.
14	Close right foot to left foot, continuing to turn partner to her right.	Step forward on left foot, making a rapid ½ turn right to face partner.
15	Step to side on left foot, resuming Closed Position.	Step to side on right foot, resuming Closed Position.
16	Close right foot to left foot.	Close left foot to right foot.

Count 1

Count 2

Count 6

Count 8

Count 9

Count 10

Count 11

Count 12

Count 13

The Gaity Polka ARRANGED BY Allen Dodworth.

NEW YORK.
FIRTH. POND & Cº Nº 1 FRANKLIN SQUARE.

The Ballroom Polka

¢ ♩ ♩ ♩ ♩ | ♩ ♩ ♩ ♩
  >   >

Although the original polka was in 2/4 time, it is almost always played in a four-count "cut" time now, with a strong accent on the first beat of each measure. The polka is a fast dance, and there are almost as many versions as there are polka dancers. It is often done as a folk dance even today, and different styles are found in Chicago, Detroit, and other parts of the country. At a Polish wedding, you may see many varieties being danced at one time as the couples hop gaily along Line of Dance with frequent long steps and many turns. Some will do a chicken hop with much bending and turning. Sometimes all the dancers will form a circle, and side-by-side couples will follow the patterns of the domino polka, both partners dancing on the same foot. In this book we give a ballroom version of polka that follows normal Line of Dance and is not likely to create traffic problems on a conventional dance floor.

The primary characteristic of the polka is the *hop*, which is always done on the upbeat. This may be an actual jump on the supporting foot, but even a slight lift of the heel of the supporting foot will qualify as long as both partners follow a similar style. Each of the figures that follow begins on the downbeat. While many dancers start the polka with a preliminary hop taken on the upbeat — *before* the first actual measure of dancing — most find it easier to begin the dance with the man's left foot (woman's right) on the strong first beat of the measure as in other ballroom dances.

Also characteristic of the polka is a continuous rise-and-fall of the body resulting from alternate steps on the flat and ball of the feet. Posture is relatively unimportant. Polka is a lively dance which relieves tension and gets the blood circulating — we welcome its return to the world of ballroom dancing.

Ballroom Polka Figure No. 1
Forward Basic

2/2 ("cut") time
Recommended measures per minute:
50–66
2 measures or 8 musical counts

COUNT	MAN'S PART	WOMAN'S PART
1	FLAT: From Closed Position, step forward on left foot directly on *downbeat* — with a light, bouncing motion (knees soft).	FLAT: Step back on right foot and lower to heel — with a light, bouncing motion (knees soft).
2	BALL: Close right foot to left foot.	BALL: Close left foot to right foot.
3	FLAT: Short step forward on left foot.	FLAT: Short step back on right foot and lower to heel.
4	HOP on left foot (even a slight lift of heel can be called a *hop*, but partners should follow the same style) — free foot is raised no more than ankle high.	HOP on right foot (even a slight lift of heel can be called a *hop*, but partners should follow the same style) — free foot is raised no more than ankle high.
5	FLAT: Step forward on right foot.	FLAT: Step back on left foot and lower to heel.
6	BALL: Close left foot to right foot.	BALL: Close right foot to left foot.
7	FLAT: Short step forward on right foot.	FLAT: Short step back on left foot and lower to heel.
8	HOP on right foot.	HOP on left foot.

Count 1

Count 2

Count 3

Count 4

Count 5

Count 6

Count 7

Count 8

Ballroom Polka Figure No. 2
Left Turning Basic

2/2 ("cut") time
Recommended measures per minute:
50–66
2 measures or 8 musical counts

COUNT	MAN'S PART	WOMAN'S PART
1	FLAT: From Closed Position, step to side on left foot, beginning ¼ turn left (to be completed in three steps).	FLAT: Step to side on right foot, beginning ¼ turn left (to be completed in three steps).
2	BALL: Close right foot to left foot as you continue to turn left.	BALL: Close left foot to right foot as you continue to turn left.
3	FLAT: Step forward on left foot, completing turn left.	FLAT: Step back on right foot and lower to heel as you complete turn left.
4	HOP on left foot.	HOP on right foot.
5	FLAT: Step to side on right foot, beginning ¼ turn left (to be completed in three steps).	FLAT: Step to side on left foot, beginning ¼ turn left (to be completed in three steps).
6	BALL: Close left foot to right foot as you continue to turn left.	BALL: Close right foot to left foot as you continue to turn left.
7	FLAT: Step back on right foot and lower to heel as you complete turn left.	FLAT: Step forward on left foot, completing turn left.
8	HOP on right foot.	HOP on left foot.

The Right Turning Basic figure is done in the same manner, with the man stepping back on Count 3 and forward on Count 7. The woman does the counterpart. Both partners turn to right during Counts 1–3 and Counts 5–7. As you become more familiar with the polka, you will also enjoy doing ½ turns left or right.

Count 1

Count 2

Count 3

Count 4

Count 5

Count 6

Count 7

Count 8

Ballroom Polka Figure No. 3
Promenade

2/2 ("cut") time
Recommended measures per minute:
50–66
2 measures or 8 musical counts

COUNT	MAN'S PART	WOMAN'S PART
1	FLAT: From Closed Position, step to side on left foot, opening into Promenade Position.	FLAT: Step to side on right foot, opening into Promenade Position.
2	BALL: Close right foot to left foot.	BALL: Close left foot to right foot.
3	FLAT: Short step forward on left (outside) foot.	FLAT: Short step forward on right (outside) foot.
4	HOP on left foot.	HOP on right foot.
5	FLAT: Step forward on right (inside) foot.	FLAT: Step forward on left (inside) foot.
6	BALL: Close left foot to right foot.	BALL: Close right foot to left foot.
7	FLAT: Short step forward on right foot.	FLAT: Short step forward on left foot.
8	HOP on right foot.	HOP on left foot.

Count 1

Count 2

Count 3

Count 4

Count 5

Count 6

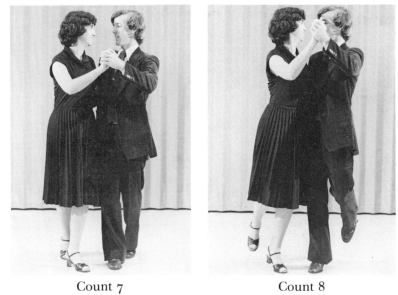
Count 7

Count 8

Ballroom Polka Figure No. 4
Arch Turn for the Woman

2/2 ("cut") time
Recommended measures per minute:
50–66
2 measures or 8 musical counts

COUNT	MAN'S PART	WOMAN'S PART
1	FLAT: From Promenade Position (following Figure No. 3), step to side on left foot, raising left hand to turn partner's right hand in an *arch* over her head as your right hand leads her into first step of a full turn to her right.	FLAT: Step forward on right foot, beginning a full turn to right under the *arch* (the first step in a small circle to be completed in eight musical counts).
2	BALL: Close right foot to left foot, continuing to turn partner to her right.	BALL: Close left foot to right foot as you continue turning right.
3	FLAT: Step to side on left foot as you continue turning partner.	FLAT: Short step forward on right foot as you continue turning to right.
4	HOP on left foot as you continue turning partner.	HOP on right foot as you continue turning to right.
5	FLAT: Close right foot to left foot as you continue turning partner.	FLAT: Short step forward on left foot as you continue turning to right.
6	BALL: Step to side on left foot as you continue turning partner.	BALL: Close right foot to left foot as you continue turning to right.
7	FLAT: Close right foot to left foot as you lead partner to complete her turn and face you.	FLAT: Short step forward on left foot as you complete turn right to face partner.
8	HOP on right foot, resuming Closed Position.	HOP on left foot, resuming Closed Position.

Count 1   Count 2   Count 3

Count 4   Count 5   Count 6

Count 7   Count 8

Ballroom Polka Figure No. 5
Heel-and-Toe

2/2 ("cut") time
Recommended measures per minute:
50–66
4 measures or 16 musical counts

COUNT	MAN'S PART	WOMAN'S PART
1	From Promenade Position, touch left HEEL forward (no weight).	Touch right HEEL forward (no weight).
2	HOP on right foot.	HOP on left foot.
3	Cross left foot in front of right foot and tap left TOE.	Cross right foot in front of left foot and tap right TOE.
4	HOP on right foot.	HOP on left foot.
5	FLAT: Step to side on left foot, turning right to Closed Position.	FLAT: Step to side on right foot, turning left to Closed Position.
6	BALL: Close right foot to left foot.	BALL: Close left foot to right foot.
7	FLAT: Step to side on left foot, turning right to Counter Promenade Position.	FLAT: Step to side on right foot, turning left to Counter Promenade Position.
8	HOP on left foot.	HOP on right foot.
9	Touch right HEEL forward (no weight).	Touch left HEEL forward (no weight).
10	HOP on left foot.	HOP on right foot.
11	Cross right foot in front of left foot and tap right TOE.	Cross left foot in front of right foot and tap left TOE.
12	HOP on left foot.	HOP on right foot.
13	FLAT: Step to side on right foot, turning left to Closed Position.	FLAT: Step to side on left foot, turning right to Closed Position.
14	BALL: Close left foot to right foot.	BALL: Close right foot to left foot.
15	FLAT: Step to side on right foot.	FLAT: Step to side on left foot.
16	HOP on right foot.	HOP on left foot.

Count 1

Count 3

Count 6

Count 7

Count 9

Count 11

Count 13

Count 14

Count 16

The Hustle

The hustle is written in 4/4 time with an accent on the first beat of each measure. Present versions of the dance are done to a six-count rhythm, as if it were simply a six-count Lindy done to disco music. As you can see, however, a measure of hustle music consists essentially of a syncopated two-beat "samba" count plus a half note. This produces uneven phrasing in a six-count dance done to four-beat music. For example, the *triple* (one half, one half, one count) in the Latin Hustle Basic (Figure No. 6) is done alternately to the syncopated "samba" count and to the half note. For this reason, most versions of the hustle appear to be danced "against the music" and represent quite a challenge to the beginner.

All forms of hustle are characterized by the *touch* or *tap* step, frequent separation of partners, and much intertwining of the arms. Following are several figures of the relatively easy American hustle and also basic figures for the *Latin hustle, Lindy hustle*, and one version of the *three-count hustle*.

Hustle Figure No. 1 (American)
The Basic

4/4 time
Recommended measures per minute:
26–32
1½ measures or 6 musical counts

COUNT	MAN'S PART	WOMAN'S PART
1	From Closed Position, *tap* to side with left foot (weight remains on right foot and knees are soft).	*Tap* to side with right foot (weight remains on left foot and knees are soft).
2	Close left foot to right foot (transfer weight to left foot).	Close right foot to left foot (transfer weight to right foot).
3	*Tap* to side with right foot (weight remains on left foot).	*Tap* to side with left foot (weight remains on right foot).
4	Close right foot to left foot (transfer weight to right foot).	Close left foot to right foot (transfer weight to left foot).
5	Step in place on left foot.	Step in place on right foot.
6	Step in place on right foot.	Step in place on left foot.

Count 1

Count 2

Count 3

Count 4

Count 5

Count 6

Hustle Figure No. 2 (American)
Spot Turn

4/4 time
Recommended measures per minute:
26–32
1½ measures or 6 musical counts

COUNT	MAN'S PART	WOMAN'S PART
1–2	From Closed Position, tap and close left foot to right foot, transferring weight to left foot.	Tap and close right foot to left foot, transferring weight to right foot.
3	Tap to side with right foot.	Tap to side with left foot.
4	Step forward on right foot with toe pointing between partner's feet.	Step back on left foot.
5	Step forward on left foot, beginning ½ turn right (clockwise).	Step back on right foot, beginning ½ turn right (clockwise).
6	Close right foot to left foot, completing turn to right.	Close left foot to right foot, completing turn to right.

Count 1

Count 2

Count 3

Count 4

Count 5

Count 6

Hustle Figure No. 3 (American)
Breakaway

4/4 time
Recommended measures per minute:
26–32
1½ measures or 6 musical counts

COUNT	MAN'S PART	WOMAN'S PART
1–2	From Closed Position, tap and close left foot to right foot, transferring weight to left foot.	Tap and close right foot to left foot, transferring weight to right foot.
3	Tap to side with right foot.	Tap to side with left foot.
4	Close right foot to left foot, removing right hand from partner's back and lowering left hand to lead her away from you into Open Break Position.	Step back on left foot.
5	Step in place on left foot, taking partner's left hand in your right for a *four-hand hold*.	Step back on right foot.
6	Step in place on right foot.	Close left foot to right foot.

Count 1

Count 2

Count 3

Count 4

Count 5

Count 6

Hustle Figure No. 4 (American)
The Pretzel

4/4 time
Recommended measures per minute:
26–32
4½ measures or 18 musical counts

COUNT	MAN'S PART	WOMAN'S PART
1–6	Complete all counts of Hustle Breakaway (Figure No. 3).	Same.
7–8	Tap and close left foot to right foot.	Tap and close right foot to left foot.
9	Tap to side with right foot.	Tap to side with left foot.
10	Close right foot to left foot, raising left hand and turning it loosely inside partner's right hand as your right hand draws her into first step of ½ turn to her left to side-by-side position.	Step diagonally forward on left foot, beginning ½ turn left (the first of two steps to side-by-side position).
11	Step in place on left foot as you lead partner around to complete her ½ turn (your right arm is now across her back with her left hand in your right at her right waist, her right hand in your left at her left waist).	Step forward on right foot, completing turn left into side-by-side position.
12	Step in place on right foot.	Close left foot to right foot.
13–14	Tap and close left foot to right foot.	Tap and close right foot to left foot.
15	Tap to side with right foot (directly behind partner's left foot).	Tap to side with left foot (directly in front of partner's right foot).
16	Close right foot to left foot, raising left hand to lead partner into first step of ½ turn to her left to face you again.	Step diagonally forward on left foot, beginning ½ turn left (the first of two steps to face partner again).
17	Step in place on left foot as you lead partner around to complete her turn left and resume Closed Position.	Step forward on right foot, completing turn left and resuming Closed Position.
18	Step in place on right foot.	Close left foot to right foot.

Count 9

Count 10

Count 12

Count 13

Count 14

Count 15

Count 16

Count 17

Count 18

Hustle Figure No. 5 (American)
The Snake

4/4 time
Recommended measures per minute:
26–32
4½ measures or 18 musical counts

COUNT	MAN'S PART	WOMAN'S PART
1–6	Complete all counts of Hustle Breakaway (Figure No. 3).	Same.
7	Tap to side with left foot, swiveling on *right* foot in ⅛ turn right.	Tap to side with right foot, swiveling on *left* foot in ⅛ turn right.
8	Cross left foot in front of right foot.	Cross right foot in back of left foot.
9	Tap to side with right foot, swiveling on *left* foot in ¼ turn left.	Tap to side with left foot, swiveling on *right* foot in ¼ turn left.
10	Cross right foot in front of left foot.	Cross left foot in back of right foot.
11	Cross left foot in front of right foot.	Cross right foot in back of left foot.
12	Cross right foot in front of left foot.	Cross left foot in back of right foot.
13	Tap to side with left foot, swiveling on *right* foot in ⅛ turn left.	Tap to side with right foot, swiveling on *left* foot in ⅛ turn left.
14	Cross left foot in back of right foot.	Cross right foot in front of left foot.
15	Tap to side with right foot, swiveling on *left* foot in ¼ turn right.	Tap to side with left foot, swiveling on *right* foot in ¼ turn right.
16	Cross right foot in back of left foot.	Cross left foot in front of right foot.
17	Cross left foot in back of right foot.	Cross right foot in front of left foot.
18	Cross right foot in back of left foot.	Cross left foot in front of right foot.

Count 7

Count 8

Count 9

Count 10

Count 11

Count 12

Count 13

Count 14

Count 15

The Basic

4/4 time
Recommended measures per minute:
26–32
1½ measures or 6 musical counts

COUNT	MAN'S PART	WOMAN'S PART
1	ONE: From Closed Position, touch left toe in back — no weight (one full count).	ONE: Touch right toe in back — no weight (one full count).
2	TWO: Step to side on left foot (one full count).	TWO: Step to side on right foot (one full count).
3	THREE: Take short step back on right foot (½ count), AND close left foot to right foot — Open Break Position optional (½ count).	THREE: Take short step back on left foot (½ count), AND close right foot to left foot (½ count).
4	FOUR: Take short step forward on right foot (one full count).	FOUR: Take short step forward on left foot (one full count).
5	FIVE: Close left foot to right foot (one full count).	FIVE: Close right foot to left foot (one full count).
6	SIX: Step in place on right foot (one full count).	SIX: Step in place on left foot (one full count).

Count 1: ONE   Count 2: TWO   Count 3 (a): THREE

Count 3 (b): AND   Count 4: FOUR

Count 5: FIVE   Count 6: SIX

Hustle Figure No. 7 (Lindy)
The Basic

4/4 time
Recommended measures per minute:
26–32
1½ measures or 6 musical counts

COUNT	MAN'S PART	WOMAN'S PART
1	ONE: From Closed Position, cross left foot in back of right foot, opening into Promenade Position (½ count), AND step in place on right foot (½ count).	ONE: Cross right foot in back of left foot, opening into Promenade Position (½ count), AND step in place on left foot (½ count).
2	TWO: Step to side on left foot into Closed Position (one full count).	TWO: Step to side on right foot into Closed Position (one full count).
3	THREE: Cross right foot in back of left foot, opening into Counter Promenade Position (½ count), AND step in place on left foot (½ count).	THREE: Cross left foot in back of right foot, opening into Counter Promenade Position (½ count), AND step in place on right foot (½ count).
4	FOUR: Step to side on right foot into Closed Position (one full count).	FOUR: Step to side on left foot into Closed Position (one full count).
5	FIVE: Step in place on left foot (one full count).	FIVE: Step in place on right foot (one full count).
6	SIX: Step in place on right foot (one full count).	SIX: Step in place on left foot (one full count).

Count 1 (a): ONE

Count 1 (b): AND

Count 2: TWO

Count 3 (a): THREE

Count 3 (b): AND

Count 4: FOUR

Count 5: FIVE

Count 6: SIX

Hustle Figure No. 8
  (Three-Count)

The Basic

4/4 time
Recommended measures per minute: 26–32
¾ measure or 3 musical counts

COUNT	MAN'S PART	WOMAN'S PART
1	AND: From Open Break Position with four-hand hold, rock back on left foot (½ count), ONE: Replace weight on right foot (½ count).	AND: Rock back on right foot (½ count), ONE: Replace weight on left foot (½ count).
2	TWO: Rock forward on left foot (one full count).	TWO: Rock forward on right foot (one full count).
3	THREE: Replace weight on right foot (one full count).	THREE: Replace weight on left foot (one full count).

Count 1 (a): AND

Count 1 (b): ONE

Count 2: TWO

Count 3: THREE

IV

BALLROOM DANCING
FOR YOU

You will soon get to know the places in your area where ballroom dancers find the best music, a good dance floor, and attractive surroundings. You will find yourself making a phone call in advance to ask whether or not a restaurant has dancing (specifically "waltzes, tangos, cha-chas," and so forth) before you decide to make a dinner reservation. When you do find a good spot, comparing notes with other dancers at "break" time will help you locate still more places.

If you are planning to hold a dance, remember that the better-known dance bands often serve as entertainment agencies today. If you do *not* want a vocalist or a "show," you must decide this in advance. Be sure to request a group of three or four musicians who *usually* play ballroom dance music (again, specify waltzes, tangos, lively fox-trots, merengues, and so forth). Many groups who claim to "play everything" prefer — after a token fox-trot and rumba — to show off their renditions of the Top 40 and, unless you are firm, that's what you will get. Once you have found the right musicians, it is wise to reserve them well in advance. Here again, you will soon develop favorites.

It is also important to remember that most records, tapes, and live musical performances are covered by the United States copyright law. Permission to use copyright material is handled by the American Society of Composers, Authors, and Publishers (ASCAP), One Lincoln Plaza, New York, New York 10023. A license fee must be paid for any public performance, defined by the new copyright law as "to perform at a place open to the public or at any place where a substantial number of persons outside of a normal circle of a family and its social acquaintances is gathered." In practice, the fee is assessed to the individual who profits from the performance, usually the owner of a restaurant where it takes place. The subject is fairly complex, and the owner of a restaurant usually refers the matter to his attorney.

A second organization which handles performing rights for musical compositions is Broadcast Music, Inc. (BMI), 40 West 57th Street, New York, New York 10019. They have become increasingly active in recent years and now control a large number of music copyrights. A less active organization is SESAC, Inc., 10 Columbus Circle, New York, New York 10019. The whole situation is rather unsatisfactory, since the owner of a large restaurant may find himself having to negotiate with three different organizations for permission to play live music.

There are exceptions to the copyright law. Educational institutions, churches, charitable organizations, and non-profit groups may use copyright material without charge. Social clubs, dance teachers, business groups, and so forth, fall into a gray area; theoretically, they are not exempt from the copyright law, but in practice the law is seldom enforced in their case. In view of this, a group of serious ballroom dancers who wish to hold their own dances may consider incorporation as a non-profit organization.

For your practice sessions or dance parties in your home, you will probably begin a collection of good dance recordings. A word of caution here: although many "oldies" are going to be on your list of favorites, everything left over from the Big Band Era is not great dance music. Every year produces a couple of new favorites for ballroom dancers, and you will soon learn how to evaluate new recordings for their danceability. Since the best dance music is often hard to find, and since records do wear out, it is a good idea to put your favorites on tapes as soon as convenient.

You do not have to buy albums of brand new recordings of "collector's items"; in fact, many of these are disappointing, particularly those that are "recreated in stereo." Many an old record in excellent condition may be found marked "50¢" at a tag sale — but always check for tell-tale surface scratches. At the end of this chapter is a list that will help you begin your search in the record shops, Salvation Army stores, church rummage sales, and so forth.

Many dancers and instructors use records produced specifically for ballroom dance instruction, such as those by Roper, Hoctor, and Arthur Murray. These are adequate and some, such as the early Roper recordings, are quite good. However, these albums vary considerably in quality and it is also tiresome to listen continuously to the same style of music.

As you become gradually addicted (this is the right word) to ballroom dancing, you may want to continue your dance instruction. For the names of reputable instructors, we suggest that you contact either Dance Educators of America or Dance Masters of America (addresses are given in the bibliography). If you are serious about dancing, you may decide to join these organizations yourself, and you will find that this book has put you well on the way to passing their entrance tests. In fact, a good deal of our basic material, particularly the terminology, is similar to that given in publications of DEA, DMA, and their parent organization, the National Council of Dance Teachers, Inc.

It is also possible that you will become interested in International, a more formalized style of ballroom dancing. Alignment is of great importance (a 180-degree turn, for example must be exact). Step patterns are precisely identified and terminology is fixed. Boards of examination are well organized, objective, and strict. The definitive text on International-style dancing is *Ballroom Dancing*, by Alex Moore; further information may be obtained from the Imperial Society of Teachers of Dancing, 70 Gloucester Place, London W 1, England. The influence of International seems to be growing throughout the United States. You are sure to hear more of it.

Following is a list of popular recordings that we have found particularly enjoyable and suitable for both instruction and social dancing. Some are available in record stores and others can be obtain only by "scrounging." Often two or three first-rate selections will be found on a single record, and some of them are real gold mines!

WALTZ

"He'll Have to Go" — Billy Vaughn, 26 mpm (DOT DLP 3322)
"Funny, Familiar, Forgotten Feeling" — Tom Jones vocal, 29 mpm (London XPAS 71062)
"Almost Persuaded" — Ray Anthony, 32 mpm (Ranwood R 8059)
"Quentin's Theme" — Lawrence Walk, 33 mpm (Ranwood R 8060)
"Funny Face" — Donna Fargo vocal, 33 mpm (Goldies 45: P2728)
"Around the World in 80 Days" — Billy Vaughn, 34 mpm (DOT DLP 25119)
"Fascination" — Lawrence Welk, 34 mpm (Ranwood R 8044)
Medley: "What'll I Do?"
        "Alice Blue Gown"
        "Three O'Clock in the Morning" — Enoch Light, 34½ mpm
        (Project PR 5086 SD)

"Together" — Ken Griffin organ, 34½ mpm (Columbia CS 8781)
"Try to Remember" — Guy Lombardo, 34½ mpm (Capital STT 2559)
"Tennessee Waltz" — Guy Lombardo, 36 mpm (Capitol T 1738)
"Somewhere My Love" — Roper Dance Orchestra, 37 mpm (Roper RRLPS 1010)
"The Last Waltz" — Engelbert Humperdinck, 37 mpm (Parrot 45: 5N-59037)
"Anniversary Waltz" — Ken Griffin organ, 37½ mpm (Columbia CS 8781)

"Chipmunk Song" — Billy Vaughn, 43 mpm (DOT DLP 25201)
"Good Night, Irene" — Joann Castle piano, 44 mpm (Ranwood RLP 8013)

FOX-TROT

"Green, Green Grass of Home" — Skitch Henderson, 24½ mpm (Columbia CS 9475)
"Make the World Go Away" — Billy Vaughn, 25 mpm (DOT DLP 3698)
"Raindrops Keep Fallin'" — B. J. Thomas, 27 mpm (Scepter SPS 580)
"Have You Ever Been Lonely?" — David Carroll, 27½ mpm (Mercury SRW 12508)
"Paper Roses" — Billy Vaughn, 29 mpm (DOT DLP 3322)
"Cold, Cold Heart" — Joann Castle piano, 31 mpm (Ranwood RLP 8013)
"Another Somebody Done Somebody Wrong Song" — B. J. Thomas, 32 mpm (Goldies 45: P2774)
"Candida" — Lawrence Welk, 33 mpm (Ranwood R 8083)
"Third Man Theme" — Jerry Burke organ, 33 mpm (Ranwood RLP 8009)
"Save the Last Dance for Me" — The Righteous Brothers, 33 mpm (Verve V6-5004)
"Wheels" — Billy Vaughn, 33 mpm (DOT DLP 3366)
"I Get the Blues When it Rains" — Ray Anthony, 33½ mpm (Ranwood R 8082)
"I Left My Heart in San Francisco" — Peter Duchin, 34½ mpm (Decca DL 74373)
"Ramblin' Rose" — Joann Castle piano, 35 mpm (DOT DLP 25511)
"My Heart Stood Still" — Artie Shaw's 1939 original, 37½ mpm (RCA CAS 465e)
"Pavanne" — Glenn Miller's 1939 original, 41½ mpm (RCA Victor LPM 1190)
"Oh, Lonesome Me!" — Al Hirt trumpet, 43 mpm (GWP ST 2005)

LINDY

"Tuxedo Junction" — Billy Vaughn, 31 mpm (DOT DLP 25288)
"Honky Tonk" — Ray Anthony, 31 mpm (Ranwood R 8082)
"The Last Blues Song" — Helen Reddy, 31 mpm (Capitol ST 11068)
"Knock Three Times" — Dawn, 32 mpm (Flashback FLB 66)
"Night Train" — Jonah Jones, 32 mpm (Capitol T 1039)
"Kansas City" — Ray Anthony, 33 mpm (Ranwood R 8082)
"Perdido" — Duke Ellington, 34 mpm (RCA VPM 6042)
"Mame" — Guy Lombardo, 34 mpm (Capitol ST 2639)
"Music Makers" — Harry James' original, 36 mpm (Capitol M-1515)
"Chattanooga Choo-Choo" — Glenn Miller, 37 mpm (RCA ANL 1-0974e)

"Look What They've Done to My Song" — Lawrence Welk, 38 mpm (Ranwood R 8083)
"Hello, Dolly!" — Herb Alpert, 39 mpm (A & M Sp 3521)
"Sugar Lips" — Al Hirt trumpet, 42 mpm (RCA Victor LSP 2965)
"In the Mood" — Glenn Miller's 1939 original, 43 mpm (RCA Victor LM 6088)
"Little Brown Jug" — Glenn Miller's 1939 original, 43 mpm (RCA Victor LPM 1506)
"Take the 'A' Train" — Duke Ellington, 44 mpm (RCA VPM 6042)
"Rosalie" — Artie Shaw 1939, 44 mpm (RCA CAS 465e)
"Woodchoppers' Ball" — Billy Vaughn, 46 mpm (DOT DLP 25201)

RUMBA

"Yellow Bird" — Lawrence Welk, 27 mpm (DOT DLP 25812)
"Two Spanish Eyes" — Al Martino vocal, 28 mpm (Capitol T 2435)
"A Man Without Love" — Billy Vaughn, 28½ mpm (DOT DLP 3882)
"Rumba Rhapsody" — The Dancing Strings for Roper, 29 mpm (Roper 45: 224A)
"Yours" — Billy Vaughn, 30 mpm (Pickwick 33 SPC 3074)
"Sorrento" — Billy Vaughn, 31 mpm (DOT DLP 3366)
"Adios, Mariquita Linda" — Billy Vaughn, 32 mpm (DOT DLP 25625)
"Rumba Maria" — Roper Dance Orchestra, 34 mpm (Roper RRLPS 1007)
"Lamento Borincano" — Roper Dance Orchestra, 34 mpm (Roper RRLPS 1006)
"Siboney" — Edmundo Ros, 40 mpm (London SP 44080)

CHA-CHA

"Something Stupid" — Skitch Henderson, 27 mpm (Columbia CS 9475)
"Rico Vacilon" — Lester Lanin, 29 mpm (Phillips PHS 600-145)
"Corazon de Melon" — Billy Vaughn, 30 mpm (DOT DLP 25625)
Medley: "I Talk to the Trees"
        "Downtown"
        "We'll Sing in the Sunshine" — Lester Lanin, 31 mpm (Phillips PHS 600-181)

"Tea for Two" — Tommy Dorsey, 31 mpm (MCA 60015)
"Tea for Two Cha-Cha No. 2" — Tommy Dorsey, 31 mpm (MCA 60015)
"Never on Sunday" — Frank Chacksfield, 31 mpm (London CHA S-1)
"Jada" — Victor Gerard for Arthur Murray, 31 mpm (RCA LSP 2998)
"Patricia" — Hugo Montenegro, 34 mpm (Time 52018)

MAMBO

"Linda Mujer" — George Barnes, 34½ mpm (Mercury PPS 6011)
"Papa Loves Mambo" — Nat King Cole vocal, 41½ mpm (Capital DF 504)
"Tequila" — Billy Vaughn, 44 mpm (DOT DLP 25201 *or* Pickwick SPC 3074)
"Caper of the Golden Bulls" — Vic Mizzy, 46 mpm (Tower ST 5086)
"Jambalaya" — Pete Fountain clarinet, 47 mpm (Coral CRL 57473)
"Mambo Jambo" — Billy Vaughn, 50 mpm (DOT DLP 25265)

TANGO

"Tango of the Roses" — Al Caiola, 24½ mpm (Roulette SR 42008)
"Den Geoso" — Nick Arnold, 26½ mpm (Coronet CX77)
"Chitarra Romana" — Al Caiola, 26½ mpm (Roulette SR 42008)
"Cherry Pink and Apple Blossom White" — Billy Vaughn, 26½ mpm (DOT DLP 25016)
"El Choclo" — Nick Arnold, 26½ mpm (Coronet CX77)
"Blue Tango" — Billy Vaughn, 27 mpm (DOT DLP 25016)
"La Cumparsita" — Enoch Light, 27½ mpm (Project PR 5086 SD)
"Hernando's Hideaway" — Billy Vaughn, 27½ mpm (DOT DLP 25201)

SAMBA

"Delicado" — Edmundo Ros, 51 mpm (London SP 44107)
"Age of Aquarius" — Xavier Cugat, 52 mpm (Decca DL 74799)
"Playtime in Brazil" — Roper Dance Orchestra, 58 mpm (Roper RRLPS 1010)
"Come to the Mardi Gras" — Xavier Cugat, 60 mpm (Columbia 37556)
"Brazil" — Xavier Cugat, 61 mpm (Columbia "Lucky Strike Special")
"Laughing Samba" — Edmundo Ros, 62 mpm (London SP 44080)
"Fools Rush In" — Lawrence Welk, 62 mpm (DOT DLP 25552)
"Heartaches" — Edmundo Ros, 62 mpm (London SP 44080)
"La Golondrina" — Edmundo Ros, 62 mpm (London SP 44073)

BOSSA NOVA

"On a Clear Day" — Xavier Cugat, 27 mpm (Decca DL 75046)
"The Girl from Ipanema" — Al Hirt trumpet, 28 mpm (RCA Victor LSP 2965)
"Theme from Elvira Madigan" — Xavier Cugat, 29 mpm (Decca DL 75046)
"Quien Sera" — Billy Vaughn, 30 mpm (DOT DLP 25625)
"Wave" — Xavier Cugat, 30 mpm (Decca DL 75046)
"Do You Know the Way?" — Xavier Cugat, 34 mpm (Decca DL 75046)

"What Kind of Fool?" — Enoch Light, 37 mpm (Command RS 851 S-D)

"Blame it on the Bossa Nova" — Edmundo Ros, 44 mpm (London SP 44073)

"Meditation" — Enoch Light, 42 mpm (Command RS 851 S-D)

"Desafinado" — Herb Alpert, 44 mpm (A & M SP 101)

MERENGUE

"Not too Fast" — Roper Dance Orchestra, 57 mpm (Roper RRLPS 1010)

"Compadre Pedro Juan" — Roper Dance Orchestra, 62 mpm (Roper RRLPS 1007)

"El Negrito del Batey" — Lester Lanin, 64 mpm (Phillips PHS 600-145)

"Chui Chui" — Latin All Stars, 64 mpm (Roper RRLPS 1021)

"Merengue Mi Amor" — Roper Dance Orchestra, 65 mpm (Roper RRLPS 1025)

POLKA

"Peanuts" — Herb Alpert, 55 mpm (A & M SP 4110)

"Just Because" — Lawrence Welk for *Reader's Digest*, 62 mpm (RCA Custom RD4-59-3)

"Hot Foot" — Lawrence Welk, 62 mpm (DOT DLP 25303)

"Helena" — Lawrence Welk for *Reader's Digest*, 63 mpm (RCA Custom RD4-59-3)

"Tic Tock" — Lawrence Welk for *Reader's Digest*, 63 mpm (RCA Custom RD4-59-3)

"Hoop Dee Doo" — Lawrence Welk for *Reader's Digest*, 64 mpm (RCA Custom RD4-59-3)

"Gilda" — Al Caiola, 65 mpm (Roulette SR 42008)

"Beer Barrel Polka" — Will Glahé 1939 original, 66 mpm (RCA Victor LM 6088)

"Just Another Polka" — Frankie Yancovic, 66 mpm (Columbia CL 974)

"Guitar Polka" — Billy Vaughn, 66 mpm (DOT DLP 3698)

HUSTLE

"Fly, Robin, Fly" — Silver Convention, 26 mpm (Midland Int'l BKL 1-2423)

"The Hustle" — Van McCoy, 29 mpm (HL 69016-698)

"Love Is the Answer" — Van McCoy, 30 mpm (HL 69016-698)

"Theme from Star Trek" — Van McCoy, 31 mpm (HL 69016-698)

"Midnight Love Affair" — Carol Douglas, 31 mpm (Midland Int'l BKL 1-2423)

BIBLIOGRAPHY

Almeida, Renato. *Historia da Musica Brasiliera*. Rio de Janeiro. 1942

Astaire, Fred. *Steps in Time*. New York: Harper & Brothers, 1958.

Butler, Albert and Josephine. *Encyclopedia of Social Dance*. The authors, New York, c. 1967.

Castle, Irene. *Castles in the Air*. Garden City: Doubleday & Co. Inc., 1958.

Castle, Irene and Vernon. *Modern Dancing*. New York: Harper & Brothers, 1914.

Cellarius. *La Danse des Salons*. The author, Paris. 1849.

Chase, Gilbert. *The Music of Spain*. New York: W. W. Norton & Company, Inc., 1941.

Courlander, Harold. *Haiti Singing*. New York: Cooper Square Publishers, Inc., 1973.

Cugat, Xavier. *Rumba Is My Life*. New York: Didier, 1942.

Dance Educators of America, Inc. *New Ballroom Syllabus*. Box 470, Caldwell, N. J. 07006, c. 1970.

Dance Masters of America, Inc. *Ballroom Teacher Training Manuals*. 723 W. Smith St., Orlando, Fla. 32804.

Dance, Stanley. *The World of Swing*. New York: Charles Scribner's Sons, 1974.

deMille, Agnes. *The Book of the Dance*. New York: Golden Press, Inc., 1963.

Dodworth, Allen. *Dancing*. New York: Harper & Brothers, 1885.

Franks, A. H. *Social Dance – a Short History*. London: Routledge and Kegan Paul, 1963.

Gammond, Peter. *Scott Joplin and the Ragtime Era*. New York: St. Martin's Press, 1975.

Green, Abel and Joe Laurie, Jr. *Show Biz*. New York: Henry Holt & Co., 1951.

Grenet, Emilio. *Popular Cuban Music*. Habana. 1939.

Hostetler, Lawrence. *The Art of Social Dancing*. New York: A. S. Barnes & Co., 1936.

Hostetler, Lawrence. *Walk Your Way to Better Dancing*. New York: A. S. Barnes & Co., 1942.

Marks, Edward B. *They All Sang*. New York: The Viking Press, 1934.

Moore, Alex. *Ballroom Dancing*. London: Pitman Publishing Ltd., 1974.

Mouvet, Maurice. *Maurice's Art of Dancing*. New York: G. Schirmer, 1915.

Murray, Arthur. *Arthury Murray's Dance Secrets*. New York, 1946.

Murray, Kathryn. *My Husband, Arthur Murray*. New York: Simon and Schuster, 1960.

Nettl, Paul. *The Story of Dance Music*. New York: Philosophical Library, 1947.

Richardson, Phillip J. S. *Social Dances of the 19th Century*. London: H. Jenkins, 1960.

Rust, Frances. *Dance in Society*. London: Routledge and Kegan Paul, 1969.

Stearns, Marshall and Jean. *Jazz Dance*. New York: Macmillan, 1968.

U. S. Ballroom Council. *Thirteen Ballroom Dances*. National Council of Dance Teacher Organizations, Inc. 1964. (available through Dance Educators of America.)

Vega, Carlos. *Danzas y Canciones Argentinas*. Buenos Aires. 1936.

Veloz, Yolanda and Frank. *Tango and Rumba*. New York: Harper & Brothers, 1938.

Vuillier, Gaston. *A History of Dancing*. New York: D. Appleton & Co., 1898.

White, Betty. *Ballroom Dancebook for Teachers*. New York: David McKay, 1962

INDEX

Albers, Mrs. Lillian, 29

Alla breve. See "Cut" time

Allemande, 7

American Ballroom Company, 54

"American Bandstand (television)," 50

American rumba: history, 43–44; music and style, 119

American rumba dance figures: Arch Turn for Woman, 122–23; Basic Rumba Box, 120–21; Cross-Body Lead to Cross Rocks to Solo Turns, 130–31; Forward Breaks, 124–25; Promenade Breaks, 126–27; Simple Wheel and Wrap-Around, 128–29

American Society of Teachers of Dancing, 38, 42

American waltz: history, 7, 13–16; music and style, 77

American waltz dance figures: Arch Turn for Woman, 84–85; Basic Waltz Box, 78–79; The Beanbag, 88–89; Forward Twinkles, 86–87; The Hesitation, 80–81; Simple Twinkle, 82–83

"Amos 'n' Andy" (radio), 49

Arch Turn: in American rumba, 122–23; in American waltz, 84–85; in ballroom polka, 210–11; basics of, 66; in cha-cha, 138; defined, 71; in fox-trot, 97; in Lindy, 107, 108–9, 110–11; in mambo, 148–49; in merengue, 200–1

Armstrong, Louis, 48

ASCAP (American Society of Composers, Authors, and Publishers), 231

Astaire, Adele, 41

Astaire, Fred, 40–41, 45

Audio Fidelity Records, 47

Backward steps, 60, 61, 65; in cha-cha, 133; in mambo, 145; in tango, 158–59

"Bal à Bougival, Le," 9

Balch, Thomas, 18

Ballard, Hank, 51

Ball change, defined, 71

Ballroom dancing: defined, 7; "genera-

tion gap" in, 55; need for economic incentives, 52, 55; revival of, 52–53, 54–55. *See also* Social dancing

Ballroom polka: history, 7, 16–19; music and style, 203

Ballroom polka dance figures: Arch Turn for Woman, 210–11; Forward Basic, 204–5; Heel-and-Toe, 212–13; Left-Turning Basic, 206–7; Promenade, 208–9

Barroso, Ary, 45

Basse dance, 4

Beatles, The, 50

Benny, Jack, 49, 50

Berlin, Irving, 30, 41

"Big band" era, 37, 48–49, 232

Black influence, 6, 25, 36, 42–43, 46, 50

Black Orpheus (motion picture), 47

"Blame It on the Bossa Nova," 47

Blythe, Vernon. *See* Castle, Vernon and Irene

BMI (Broadcast Music, Inc.), 232

Bok, Edward, 26

Bonfa, Louis, 47

Bossa nova: history, 47–48; music and style, 181

Bossa nova dance figures: Away and Together, 186–87; Forward Basic, 184–85; Samba Adaptation, 190–91; Side Basic, 182–83; Tango Adaptation, 188–89

Boston, The, 16, 77

Boswell Sisters, The, 50

Boucher, Paul, 45

"Brasil," 45

Brazil (motion picture), 45

Breakaway: in cha-cha, 142–43; in hustle, 219; in Lindy, 106; in merengue, 200–1. *See also* Open Break Position

Brecker, Lou, 52. *See also* Roseland Dance City

Brent, Evelyn, 35

Bromley, the Reverend W. H., 29

Brush: defined, 71; in fox-trot, 91, 92–93

Byron, George Gordon, Lord, 14

Café de Paris, 29, 30

"Carioca, The," 41

Carrington, Arthur. *See* Fox, Harry

Castle, Vernon and Irene, 25, 30–31, 40, 44

Castle Walk, The, 25

Catholic Church, influence of, 13

Cellarius, 17–18

Cha-cha: history, 47; music and style, 133

Cha-cha dance figures: Breakaway to Cuddles, 142–43; The Chase, 140–41; Cross Rocks to Arch Turn for Woman, 138; Cross Rocks to Solo Turns, 139; Passing Basic, 134–35; Side Basic or "Cross Rocks," 136–37

Challenge Position: basics of, 65; defined, 71; introduced in a cha-cha dance figure, 140–41

Charleston, The, 37, 44

Chassé: defined, 71; in cha-cha, 134–35; in Lindy, 112–13; in merengue, 193, 194

Chavanne, 14

Checker, Chubby, 51

Christian Century, The (magazine), 52

Clare, Sidney, 50

Clark, Dick, 50

Class distinctions, 9

Claves, 43, 119

Clendennen, F. Leslie, 35

Clooney, Rosemary, 46

Close, defined, 71

Closed-couple dances, 7

Closed Position: basics of, 58–60; defined, 71

Club El Chico, 43

Cole, Nat King, 47

Coleman, Emil, 43

Collada, Benito, 43

Commando: defined, 71; introduced in a mambo dance figure, 148–49

"Continental, The," 41

Contrary Body Movement (CBM): defined, 71, 157; introduced in a tango dance figure, 166–67

Contrary Body Movement Position (CBMP): defined, 71, 157; introduced in a tango dance figure, 158–59

Contredanse, 5, 7

Corté: defined, 7, 157; introduced in a tango dance figure, 161

Costume for ballroom dancing, 31

Cotillion, 5

Counter Promenade Position: basics of, 64; defined, 72; introduced in an American waltz dance figure, 88–89

Crawford, Joan, 41

Crosby, Bing, 41, 49

Cross-body lead, 130–31

Cross rocks: in American rumba, 130–31; in cha-cha, 136–37, 138, 139

Cuban Motion: basic technique of, 119; defined, 72; introduced in an American rumba dance figure, 120–21

Cuddle Position; basics of, 65; defined, 71; introduced in a cha-cha dance figure, 142–43

Cugat, Xavier, 44, 230

Curtis, Beatrice, 35

Cut: defined, 72, 169; introduced in a samba dance figure, 170–71

"Cut" time: in dance music, 69; defined, 72

Dance Educators of America (DEA), 71, 232

Dance Masters of America (DMA), 71, 232

Dance positions, 62–65

Dance programs, 20–21, 23

Dance recordings, 232, 233–38

Dance studios, 37–40, 41, 46

Dance Teachers' Business Association, 41, 42

Dancing and Its Relation to Education and Social Life, 10

Dancing Charts for Home Instruction, 38

"Dancing Cheek to Cheek," 41

Dancing Lady (motion picutre), 41

Dancing Times (magazine), 35

Dancing Without a Master, 38

Danse des Salons, ha, 17

Danzón, 43, 47

Definitions. *See* Terminology

Del Rio, Dolores, 45

"Desafinado," 47

Diaphragm lead, 60

Dillingham, Charles, 30

Disco, origin and history, 52–53

Dodworth, Allen, 10

Dodworth, T. George, 26

Dolly, Yansci and Roszika, 33–35

Donga, 44

Dorsey, Jimmy, 48

Dorsey, Tommy, 48

Downbeat, 6, 78, 92, 203; defined, 72

Draw: defined, 72; in American waltz, 80–81; in tango, 157, 158–59
Durang, Charles, 28
Duryea, Oscar, 35

Ellington, Duke, 37, 42, 48
"Entertainer, The," 24
"Everybody's Doing It," 25

Fan: defined, 72, 157; introduced in a tango dance figure, 162–63
Fashionable Dancer's Casket, The, 28
Faulkner, T.A., 11
Faye, Alice, 41
Figure, defined, 72
Flying Down to Rio (motion picture), 41, 45
Following, basic techniques of, 61–62
Follow the Fleet (motion picture), 41
42nd Street (motion picture), 41
Forward steps, technique of 60, 61, 65; in American waltz, 77; in cha-cha, 133; in mambo, 145; in tango, 158–59
Four-hand hold, 219
Fox, George L., 32
Fox, Harry, 32–35
Fox-trot: history, 32–36; music and style, 91
Fox-trot dance figures: The Conversation, 96; The Conversation with Arch Turn for Woman, 97; Forward Basic, 94–95; Left Rock Turns, 98–99; The Park Avenue, 100–1; Slow-Quick-Quick Basic, 102–3; Slow-Slow-Quick-Quick Basic, 92–93
Franken, Joseph, 18
Freed, Alan, 51
Free foot, defined, 72
French Revolution, influence of, 13–15
Frey, Sidney, 47
From the Ballroom to Hell, 11

Gable, Clark, 41
Galop, 18
Galoppade, wie sie getanzt werden soll, Die, 18
Gay Divorcee, The (motion picture), 41
Gershwin, George, 41
Gilberto, Joao, 47
"Girl from Ipanema, The," 47
Godey's Ladies' Book (magazine), 24
Goodman, Benny, 37, 48
Grant, Donald, 41, 42
Great Dolly Sisters, The (motion picture), 35

Haley, Bill, and the Comets, 51
Harper's Weekly (magazine), 22
Hart, Lorenz, 41
Henderson, Fletcher, 42, 48
Henie, Sonja, 41
Herman, Woody, 48
Hesitation, 16, 80–81
Hispanic influence, 5–6, 27, 43–47, 54
"Hit Parade, The" (radio), 49
Hollywood, influence of, 41
"Hustle, The," 53, 214
Hustle, American, dance figures: The Basic, 216–17; The Breakaway, 219; The Pretzel, 220–21; The Snake, 222–23; Spot Turn, 218
Hustle: history, 53–54; music and style, 215
Hustle, Latin: The Basic, 224–25
Hustle, Lindy: The Basic, 226–27
Hustle, Three-Count: The Basic, 228

Imperial Society of Teachers of Dancing, 36, 233
Industrial revolution, influence of, 11
In Gay Madrid (motion picture), 44
International Association of Masters of Dancing, 38
International (English) style, 59, 77, 91, 233
"I Saw Mommy Do the Mambo," 46
"It Don't Mean a Thing if It Ain't Got That Swing," 37

James, Harry, 48
Jazz, influence of, 36–37
Jitterbug. *See* Lindy
Jive. *See* Lindy
Jobim, Antonio Carlos, 47
Joplin, Scott, 24–25

Karl, Julian, 38
Keeler, Ruby, 41
Kent State University, 52
Kern, Jerome, 41
King, Wayne, 49
Krupa, Gene, 48

Ladies' Home Journal, 26
Lancers, 5
Lanin, Lester, 54
Lanner, Franz, 15
Lead-in, 133, 145

Leading, basic techniques of, 60–61

Lee, Peggy, 50

Left Outside Position: basics of, 63; defined, 72; introduced in an American waltz dance figure, 86–87

Lindy: history, 37, 42–43; music and style, 105

Lindy dance figures: Arch Turn for Woman to Open Break Position, 107; Arch Turn to Loop Turn for Woman, 108–9; The Mooch, 116–17; She Go, He Go, 110–11; Single Lindy Basic, 106; Sugarfoot Walk, 114–15; Triple Lindy Basic, 112–13

Line of Dance (Line of Direction), 67, 77, 91, 203; defined, 72

Lombard, Carole, 44

Lombardo, Guy, 48, 49

Loop Turn: basics of, 67; defined, 72; introduced in a Lindy dance figure, 108–9

Lunceford, Jimmy, 48, 50

McAllister, Ward, 10

McCoy, Van, 53

"Make Believe Ballroom" (radio), 49

Mambo: history, 46–47; music and style, 145

Mambo dance figures: Arch Turn for Woman, 148–49; Passing Basic, 146–47; Promenade Twist, 152–53; Solo Turns, 150–51; Swivel Basic, 154–55

"Mambo Italiano," 46

"Maple Leaf Rag," 24

Maracas, 43, 119

Marbury, Mrs. Elizabeth, 30

Marimbola, 43

Marks, Edward, Music Company, 44

Maxixe, 30, 44

Measures per minute (mpm), 70

Merengue: history, 45–46; music and style, 193

Merengue dance figures: Away and Together, 198–99; Basic *Chassé*, 194; Grapevine to Left, 196–97; Left Spot Turn to Breakaway to Wheel and Arch, 200–1; Quarter Turns, 195

Miller, Glenn, 48

Millership, Florrie, 35

Minuet, 5, 7, 9

Miranda, Carmen, 45

Modern Dancing, 30, 31

Moore, Alex, 233

Mouvet, Maurice, 27

Murray, Arthur, 32, 38–40, 50, 54, 60, 232

Murray, Kathryn, 50

Musical count, 69–70

Musical notation, 68–70

National Council of Dance Teachers, Inc., 233

National Swing Club of America, 42

New York Society of Teachers of Dancing, 43, 45

New York *Times*, 21, 32, 33, 34, 35

"Night and Day," 41

Novarro, Ramon, 44

Nutl, Paul, 42

Offbeat, *See* Weak beat

One-step, 7, 25

Open Break Position: basics of, 64; defined, 72; introduced in a Lindy dance figure, 107. *See also* Breakaway

Open Counter Promenade Position: basics of, 64; defined, 72; introduced in an American rumba dance figure, 126–27

Open-couple dances, 6

Open Promenade Position: basics of, 63; defined, 72; introduced in a cha-cha dance figure, 136–37

"Orchids in the Moonlight," 41

Over the River (revue), 25, 28

Over the Top (revue), 41

"Papa Loves Mambo," 46

Papanti, Lorenzo, 15

Park Plaza Ballroom, 46

Pavane, 3, 4

Peabody, The, 27, 36, 91

Peabody, William Frank, 36

"Peanut Vender, The," 44

"Pelo Telefone," 44

Pendulum motion, 169

Phrasing: defined, 69, 72; in cha-cha, 133; in hustle, 215; in mambo, 145

Pivot, defined, 73

Polka. *See* Ballroom polka

Porter, Cole, 41

Posture, 58, 60, 77, 91, 119

Powell, Dick, 41

Prado, Prez, 47

Presley, Elvis, 50, 51

"Princess Lily Girdle," 26

Principes du Minuet, 14

Progressive dance, defined, 73
Promenade Position: basics of, 63; defined, 73; introduced in an American waltz dance figure, 82–83

Quadrille, 5, 7
Quickstep, 36, 91
Quinn, Lew, 43

Raab (Prague dancing teacher) 18
Radio, influence of, 49–50
Raft, George, 44
Ragtime, 24–25
Reformation, influence of, 12
Renoir, Pierre Auguste, 9
Rhythm, 68; defined, 73; interchangeable, 91, 105. *See also* Timing
Richardson, P. J. S., 19
Right Outside Position: basics of, 62; defined, 73; introduced in an American waltz dance figure, 86–87
Rise-and-fall: defined, 73; in American waltz, 77; in ballroom polka, 203
RKO (Radio Keith Orpheum), 41
Roaring Twenties, 32
Roberta (motion picture), 41
Rock-and-roll, origin and history, 50–51
"Rock It for Me," 50
Rock step: defined, 73; introduced in a fox-trot dance figure, 98–99
Rodgers, Richard, 41
Rogers, Ginger, 40–41
Roseland Dance City, 4, 52. *See also* Brecker, Lou
Roseland fox-trot, 91
Rothkugel, Max, 38
Round dancing, 5, 7–8
Rumba. *See* American rumba
Rumba, Cuban style, 44
Rumba (motion picture), 44

Samba: history, 44–45; music and style, 169
Samba dance figures: *Boto Fogos*, 176–77; Brazilian Basic, 170–71; Extended Basic, 172–73; Samba Walk in Promenade, 174–75' Twinkles with Extended Basic, 178–79
Savoy Ballroom, 42
Sawyer, Joan, 43
Scudder, the Reverend John, 13
Semi-open. *See* Promenade Position

SESAC, Inc., 232
Shaw, Artie, 48
Sinatra, Frank, 50
Skating Position. *See* Cuddle Position
"Smoke Gets in Your Eyes," 41
Snowden, "Shorty George," 42
Social Dances of the 19th Century, 19
Social dancing and the clergy, 12–13; defined, 4; as exercise, 32; as target of reformers, 7–8, 11–15, 26. *See also* Ballroom dancing
Solo Turns: in American rumba, 130–31; basics of, 67; in cha-cha, 139; defined, 67; in mambo, 150–51
Son, 43
Sousa, John Philip, 19
Spin, defined, 73
Spot dance, defined, 73
Spot Turn, defined, 73
Staccato, defined, 73
Step, defined, 65, 73
Steps, basic technique of, 60, 61, 65
Sting, The (motion picture), 24
Story of Vernon and Irene Castle, The (motion picture), 41
Strauss, Johann, 13, 15, 77
Strong beat, 68, 145, 203
Stupak, R. J., 52
Supporting foot, defined, 73
Sway, defined, 73
Swing, 37, 42–43. *See also* Lindy
Swing Time (motion picture), 41
Swivel: defined, 73; in American hustle, 222–23; in Lindy, 114–15; in mambo, 152–53, 154–55
Syncopation, defined, 69, 73

Tango: history, 5, 7, 27–30; music and style, 157
Tango dance figures: Fan for Woman, 162–63; Forward Basic, 158–59; Left-Turning Rocks to Simple *Corté*, 166–67; Open Fan, 164–65; Outside Basic, 160; Simple *Corté* to Tango Draw, 161

Teichman, Murray. *See* Murray, Arthur
Television, influence of, 49–50
Tempo, 70; defined, 73
Tension hold, 105
Terminology, 71–73
That Night in Rio (motion picture), 45
Thé dansants, 28, 30

"They Were Doin' the Mambo," 46, 144

Time signature, 68

Times, The (London), 14

Times (New York), 21, 32, 33, 34, 35

Timing, 61, 68–70

"Top Forty," 51

Top Hat (motion picture), 41

Transatlantic Merry-Go-Round (motion picture), 50

Triple step: in cha-cha, 133; defined, 73; in Lindy, 112–13, 114–15

Turkey trot, 25–27

Turn, defined, 73

Turning basic: in American rumba, 128–29; in American waltz, 79; in ballroom polka, 206–7; in fox-trot 102; in Lindy, 106; in samba, 170

Turns, basic technique of, 66–67

Twinkle: defined, 73; introduced in an American waltz dance figure, 82–83

Twist, origin and history, 51–52

Two-step, 7, 16, 19, 36

Two-Step, The (magazine), 20

United States Ballroom Council, 71

University of Connecticut, 4, 54

Upbeat, defined, 68, 73

Vallee, Rudy, 49

Valse à deux temps, 16, 18, 19

Variety Magazine, 33–34

Varsouvienne. See Cuddle Position

Vassar College, 54

Veloz and Yolanda, 30

Viennese waltz, 77, 81; early modification of, 15

Walton, Florence, 28

Waltz. *See* American waltz, Viennese waltz

Waring, Fred, 49

"Washington Post March," 19

Watch Your Step (revue), 30

Way to Dance, The, 39

Weak beat, 68, 145

Webb, Chick, 50

Welk, Lawrence, 19, 50, 55

Werner, Kay and Sue, 50

Wheel: in American rumba, 128–29; in merengue, 200–1

Whiteman, Paul, 42, 48, 49

Whiting, Richard, 50

Whittemore, Mrs. E.M., 11

Wilson, G. Hepburn, M.B., 32

Yale University, 54

Youmans, Vincent, 41